WHEN YOU LOVE
A FUNCTIONAL
ALCOHOLIC

William F. Kraft, PhD

PAULIST PRESS
New York/Mahwah, NJ

Cover and book design by Lynn Else

Library of Congress Cataloging-in-Publication Data

Kraft, William F., 1938–
    When you love a functional alcoholic / William F. Kraft.
        p. cm.
    Includes bibliographical references (p.   ).
    ISBN 978-0-8091-4679-6 (alk. paper)
    1. Alcoholics—Family relationships. 2. Alcoholism—Religious aspects—Christianity. 3. Alcoholism—Treatment. 4. Alcoholics—Rehabilitation. 5. Recovering alcoholics—Family relationships. I. Title.
    HV5132.K733 2011
    362.292´3—dc22

                                                                                  2010030813

Published by Paulist Press
997 Macarthur Boulevard
Mahwah, New Jersey 07430

www.paulistpress.com

Printed and bound in the
United States of America

CONTENTS

Introduction vii
1. The Three A's of Change 1
2. Is Your Loved One an Alcoholic? 6
3. "How Can I Help?" 15
4. Dangerous Beliefs and Expectations 19
5. More Well-Intentioned Mistakes 26
6. Enabling 35
7. People Pleasers and Other Toxic Loves 41
8. Aggressive and Avoidant Caretakers 46
9. Spirituality: The Way to Recovery 50
10. Where Is God? 57
11. How Do You Love? 62
12. The Courageous Way of Compassion 70
13. "How Can I Forgive?" 75
14. The Strength of Humility and Gratitude 79
15. When You Feel Upset, HALT 84
16. Managing Stress 88
17. Is Communication Possible? 94
18. Setting Boundaries 98
19. Grieving Your Losses 102
20. Living with a Teenaged Drinker 106
21. A Family Problem 114
22. When You Feel Guilty and Worried 118
23. When You Feel Alone and Lonely 122

24. When You Feel Depressed, Fearful, and Anxious 126

25. Restoring Broken Trust 131

26. Learning to Care for Yourself 135

27. Getting the Help You Need 140

28. Individual Interventions 145

29. Making Amends 149

30. Dry and Sober—Now What? 152

31. Slips and Relapses 155

32. Fruits of Your Labor 159

Bibliography 162

Dedicated to the courageous people of Al-Anon,
Alcoholics Anonymous, Caduceus, and POTADA

ACKNOWLEDGMENTS

I thank Heather and Kevin for their editorial and personal support, and Pat and Cara for their secretarial help. I am also grateful to my family, friends, and God, as well as recovering people of 12-step fellowships who evoke the good, who enlighten and console, and who engender freedom and serenity.

INTRODUCTION

When you love a functional alcoholic, you are likely to feel confused and frustrated, and often alone and lonely. Because your drinker normally functions well in public, people seldom understand your personal plight. They may even expect you to be content. I wrote this book for family, friends, and others who care about people who drink too much.

Most people mistakenly assume that alcoholics are abnormal and dysfunctional. More often than not, alcoholics are publicly responsible, avoid legal trouble, maintain propriety, and have a good job and reputation, as well as friends. In their private lives, however, we will see that a very different scenario unfolds.

Furthermore, little has been written specifically about functional alcoholics, and even less about living with and helping them and yourself. Relatively dysfunctional alcoholics get the most attention and treatment. Therefore, if you care about a more functional but less recognized and treated alcoholic, this book will help you.

This book focuses on "us" rather than "them," because we cannot make an alcoholic (or anyone) healthy. We can only change ourselves. However, when we ourselves become healthier, we increase the likelihood of our loved ones becoming sober. Therefore, in this book we will discuss the nature of a functional alcoholic and its impact on you. You'll see:

- How to learn principles and strategies to improve yourself and your loved ones
- How your sincere efforts to help may actually hinder and harm your loved ones' recovery
- How to listen to and learn from your pain in ways that strengthen and enable you to hurt less and help more

- How to use psychological and social coping skills
- How to draw on spiritual resources
- How to be free and serene, regardless of what happens

As a psychologist, I emphasize the practical value of our Higher Power, for my primary concern is our spiritual life. You can call this power whatever you want: God, love, universal self, community, loved ones, Tao, the teachings of Buddhism, Judaism, Islam, Christianity, or so on. I use the word *God* to refer to the Higher Power of Uncreated Love. Since I am not a theologian, I do not include religious traditions, magisterial teachings, or theologies.

We will explain how functional alcoholics find temporary peace from a false god—spirits or alcohol. We, on the other hand, are left with the suffering that calls for an efficacious Spirit. We will see how we become weaker, more vulnerable, and less effective when we minimize, exploit, or forget about our Higher Power—God. We will also show how we can learn physical, psychosocial, and spiritual ways that enlighten, empower, liberate, and console our loved ones and us. In short, we can come to the saving and sustaining sources of recovery, always for ourselves, and often for our loved ones.

Chapter One

THE THREE A'S OF CHANGE

"Is Larry an alcoholic? I'm not sure. Listen, my dad was a mean drunk, so I know what an alcoholic is. Larry's not one of them. He's never violent, abusive, or embarrassing. Actually, if he were a drunk, it might be easier because I could act accordingly.

"Unlike my dad, Larry never misses work or goes to bars. He's good with the kids, does his share of chores, is active in church, and overall is responsible. He's a good man. People envy me, and some say that I should be grateful to be married to such a great person. And in many respects, I am. So what am I complaining about?

"My Dad would get drunk in bars, and when he finally got home, he was stone drunk and abusive to Mom, and all of us kids would hide. We knew he was an abusive alcoholic, and we learned to survive. But with Larry, it's different. Larry drinks at home and is never violent. When he does drink, which is several times a week, he is mild and mellow, and he simply goes to sleep. So what's so bad about that?

"Well, try to communicate with someone who is asleep or not 'with it.' It's like he's more in his world than in ours, and that makes a world of difference to me and the kids—to our family. Like I said, Larry is great in public and at work, but at home, he shuts down and withdraws.

"Of course, no one knows this part of our life; they just see the all-American family. On one level, things are good, but personally I feel alone and lonely. I'm confused. People say that I should be happy, but I'm sad and empty. I love Larry; it would be easier if I didn't. Am I off base?"

1

AWARENESS, ACCEPTANCE, AND ACTION

Larry's wife, Jennifer, is *not* off base. Understandably, she harbors mixed feelings as well as self-doubt. Unlike her alcoholic father, Jennifer's husband is civil as well as socially successful. Nevertheless, Larry's drinking does seriously impede their private life. Besides shutting down emotionally, he isolates and withdraws from his wife and children.

Because Larry is a far more functional drinker than her father was, Jennifer is reluctant to recognize the symptoms of her husband's drinking problem. However, until she or her husband accepts the problem for what it is, the chances for improvement are minuscule.

The three A's of recovery for our loved ones and ourselves are *awareness*, *acceptance*, and *action*. Until we allow ourselves to become aware of what is going on, we are unlikely to cope effectively. Nevertheless, in many families there is an unspoken agreement to deny the obvious, to repress feelings, and to distort reality.

Out of ignorance or fear, or both, we deny and rationalize our loved one's drinking as well as our own enabling behavior. Some of us medicate our pain, lose ourselves in work, play the victim role, try to rescue, or act out in anger. Yet the pain does not go away; in fact, it stays with us and gets stronger.

Maybe, like Jennifer, *you* are yearning to love your spouse but are feeling frustrated, lonely, hurt, and perhaps resentful. Maybe you are concerned about the effect your spouse's drinking has on your children. If so, you are not alone. Many people have questions and feelings like yours, and this book is a response to them.

Listen to Jim:

"After twenty-two years, I still love Karen, but drinking has always been my competition. I know Karen loves me, but there are times I think she loves alcohol more.

"Karen usually nurses a stiff drink while making dinner, and later in the evening when our children have retired or are in their rooms, she has another Manhattan or two or three. Although she's rarely drunk, she gets a buzz and zones out.

Then it is virtually impossible to have a decent conversation. Often, she simply goes to sleep, and several hours later she goes to bed.

"I hesitate to call her an alcoholic because overall she functions well. She never gets aggressive or argumentative. Actually, you can say that she mellows, but is far from fully present. Few if any people would call Karen an alcoholic, but I know she drinks too much. What should I do? What can I do?"

Like Jim, you may be worried that your marriage is slipping away. Although your spouse loves you, it is clear to you that he or she loves alcohol as well. In that sense, your spouse may be having an ongoing affair with alcohol. Consequently, instead of growing closer, you drift slowly and painfully apart.

You feel that something essential is missing in your marriage. Feeling that you are unable to give what your spouse needs, you may doubt yourself as an adequate spouse, lover, or friend. Consequently, your self-esteem decreases, while sense of unworthiness increases.

Your losses can engender grief and depression, and seriously compromise your trust. These and other feelings can often affect other aspects of your life, like your social life and work. Moreover, you can be leery of, and avoid, intimacy the rest of your life.

Problems like this are highly destructive to any relationship. If you are experiencing this kind of pain, it is essential that you accept your part in the problem and take corrective steps.

To admit your part does not mean that you are the cause (or the cure) of your loved one's drinking. It simply means that you can *improve*, and therefore *lessen* your pain and *increase* your serenity. Remember, the only person you can change for the better is you.

Nevertheless, it is tempting to focus on the "problem person," and claim that he or she is the sole source of our misery. However, the truth is that we, too, have probably contributed to our own unhappiness. When we are aware of and accept our part in the madness, we can do something about it. *Recognizing this fact is the first step toward positive change.*

Some of us accept that our loved one has a drinking problem, but we refuse to accept our own well-intentioned enabling and futile attempts to change the alcoholic. When we recognize how we unknowingly supported negative behavior, or conveyed consent to unacceptable behavior, we can begin to change our situation. Acceptance is the gateway to positive change. When we accept and change our part in the drinking process, life does get better.

Naming and *claiming* how we enable and try to fix our loved one opens up a new field of possibilities. Indeed, this is not easy, for admitting to our part in what we abhor takes humility and courage, yet it brings life-saving results. Now we can do something; we no longer need to be confused, frightened, or angry victims. We can change ourselves, and life can and will improve.

Besides discovering the possibilities for positive change, *acceptance* means that we can learn to live serenely with what we cannot change. We accept that we cannot change anyone else for the better, except ourselves.

We also come to realize that our loved ones do not have to change for our own lives to improve. Although we prefer and may long for him or her to become sober, we learn to live and cope with the drinker.

THE PROMISE OF POWER

When someone you love drinks too much, the world can sometimes seem dark and hopeless. We feel desperately trapped, and may despair of things ever getting better. We may falsely assume that acceptance means to give up, to be helpless, or to be unloving. Indeed, to accept that you are powerless but not helpless is easier said than done.

We will see that when we admit that we are powerless over our loved ones—when we realize we cannot control, change, or cure our loved ones—we can connect with our Higher Power. Then, amazing things can and *do* happen.

When you can accept that you have less power than you assumed or would like, you can surrender to a Higher Power that is more than a part of yourself. You realize that you are never alone.

Paradoxically, admitting your powerlessness actually liberates and *empowers* you. You open up to new possibilities of effective coping and living. You come to experience the peace and power of connecting with a Higher Power.

When your serenity is disturbed, we will show how you can go to God and others to help you accept and change what you can, and to live serenely with what is beyond your control. With your Higher Power, you can hurt much less and cope much better.

In the following chapters, we will show how we can learn to act appropriately and effectively, how we can set boundaries, love with detachment, and manage and care for loved ones and ourselves. We can learn to live in peace with the sad and disturbing reality of an excessive drinker. In the service of increasing our awareness, acceptance, and action, let us begin with understanding functional alcoholism.

Chapter Two

IS YOUR LOVED ONE AN ALCOHOLIC?

How do you know if someone you love one is an alcoholic? Could you be misjudging this person? Keep in mind that alcoholics have often convinced themselves—and are eager to convince others—that they do not have a drinking problem.

- How can you know for sure?
- What do alcoholics look like?
- Why do they drink so much?
- What do we mean when we say someone is a functional alcoholic?

The answers to such questions are very important because how you construe drinking will highly influence the way you respond to drinking and drinkers. For instance, if you view an alcoholic as someone who loses control and rages while drinking, you are apt to rationalize the behavior of functional and pleasant alcoholics.

PROFILES OF ALCOHOLICS

Let us begin by discussing what it means to be an alcoholic, and then specifically a functional alcoholic. Realize that alcoholics vary considerably in how and why they drink and that there are many kinds of alcoholics.

Some people are physically dependent on alcohol, and their addiction manifests a primary, progressive, chronic, and fatal disease. For them, one drink is too many and a thousand are not enough.

Some alcoholics get grossly out of control and become disruptive, in contrast to those who mildly fade away and pass out. Others drink too much periodically or in certain circumstances, like celebrations, but otherwise function relatively well.

Most alcoholics seldom cause blatant trouble but rather evoke more subtle and private difficulties. Publicly, most manage well, exercise control, make good choices, succeed at work, and may even evoke admiration. Yet we will see that their public lives hide a darker private side. In reality, all alcoholics cause problems for themselves and others, though they differ in kind and intensity.

Consider an alcoholic parent. Common effects on children are confusion, fear, disconnect, and distrust. Listen to John's story, as told by his adult son Paul:

"I never really got to know my Dad, never got close to him. And sadly, I don't think he knew me, either. When he wasn't working, he was drinking. He was never there for me, or for my brother and sister.

"He would promise to watch me play ball or take me somewhere, and then he wouldn't show up. Or he would say that he'd do something for me and then forget. Sometimes he would scream at me, and then an hour later apologize profusely and buy me a gift. I never knew what was going to happen. It was really confusing. In order to survive, I learned not to depend on him, to be self-sufficient to a fault.

"Friday night was his night to go out and drink. When he came home, he and Mom would argue and fight. I'd lie in bed scared and sick to my stomach. Poor Mom, she put up with so much, I guess, for our sake.

"When Dad got cirrhosis of the liver, she took care of him without complaints. She always took care of him. I wonder who took care of her."

Most alcoholics are less disruptive than Paul's dad was, though some are more violent. Listen to another adult child of a more functional alcoholic:

"We sort of knew that Dad drank too much, but he always seemed to meet his responsibilities and stay out of trouble. In spite of his drinking, he was and is a good father and grandfather. He'd probably give anything to us and his grandchildren. I guess we thought that when Pap retired, he would drink less, but when Mom died, things got worse. To compound matters, he drinks and takes medication.

"Although he is still a nice guy, we can't really trust him anymore. Although he denies it, he drinks and drives so we are reluctant to let him take the kids on trips. He's a constant worry.

"It hurts to see him go backward at a time when he could really be enjoying life. It's tragic. This man has worked hard all his life, and he's dying before his time. But what can we do?"

Problem drinking is more common among the elderly than we realize. To watch your parents or grandparents drink themselves out of your lives can be depressing. Instead of enjoying their last years with them, you begin to lose them to alcohol. Moreover, to some extent, you die with them.

So, what does it mean to be alcoholic? Let us look at what alcoholics have in common—or, what makes your loved one an alcoholic.

COMMON ALCOHOLIC PATTERNS

Although every drinker is unique, there are common patterns among them. Perhaps your loved one resembles one of these:

Classic Alcoholics

Classic alcoholics manifest a primary, progressive, chronic, and fatal disease. Their alcoholism is not secondary to or a symptom of some other disease; it is *the* primary disease. As long as they drink, their alcoholism will get worse rather than stop or get better.

Their alcoholism is also chronic in that it is irreversible; once an alcoholic, always an alcoholic. And if they continue to drink, they will die, at least psychologically and spiritually, before their time.

Since they are physically dependent on alcohol, their tolerance increases and abstinence usually evokes serious withdrawal symptoms. These alcoholics are more dysfunctional, disruptive, disconnected, dislocated, disappointing, disgusting, disingenuous, despicable, and disheartening.

These alcoholics are the ones we usually identify as alcoholics. They often cause serious trouble like alienation, betrayal, medical and economic problems, and divorce. Most alcoholics, however, are more functional than these dysfunctional drinkers are.

Periodic Alcoholics

Some alcoholics can go days, months, or years without drinking. Yet, just when you are getting used to their relative sobriety, they start to drink again. It is like living with a ticking time bomb, uncertain when it is going to explode. Even in the peaceful times, you hear it ticking.

Listen to this alcoholic abstainer:

"Every Lent I would go on the wagon. Everyone would admire me for my self-control and sacrifice. And everyone, including myself, believed the deception. To reinforce my Lenten scam, I would periodically quit drinking for several months to lose weight and to prove that I had no problem with drinking. It was as if my urge to drink was put on hold, but I knew it was always there for me to return to. To quit forever was untenable and frightening."

Closet Alcoholics

This style of drinking is a metaphor for those who are silent and secret drinkers. Since they behave well in public and are often admired, people would doubt you if you told them that your loved one is an alcoholic. They might even see *you* as the problem. Therefore, the drinker remains "in the closet," leaving you on the outside, alone and frustrated.

"Polished" Alcoholics

Many alcoholics are far from being disheveled and unruly, like the alcoholic stereotype. These alcoholics are articulate, well groomed, seemingly confident, and mentally sharp. In their public roles, they know their lines well and usually manage to give highly rated performances.

Politicians, clergy, physicians, and other professionals who abuse alcohol often cultivate the art of drinking with grace and precision while achieving relaxation for manageable and even extended times. When these drinkers happen to slip beyond the boundaries of appropriate behavior, they manage to vanish and buy time to cover up and sober up.

Borderline Alcoholics

This type of alcoholic moves back and forth between functional and dysfunctional drinking. Gradually, they lose the control and manageability that they once had. Being alcohol abusers, they may not be physically dependent on alcohol, but they continue to abuse despite serious negative consequences.

These profiles are examples of the many kinds of alcoholics. Whether or not your loved one fits any of these profiles, the result is the same. Rarely do alcoholics become sober until they are willing and able to get the help they need. Unfortunately, this often means that things will get worse before they improve.

WHAT IS ALCOHOLISM?

Alcoholism means that one has an unhealthy relationship with alcohol. The alcoholic perceives, thinks, feels about, and relates to alcohol differently than non-alcoholics do. Thus, alcoholism is not only a matter of quantity—how much one drinks; it is also a matter of motive—how and why one drinks. For instance, if your loved one consistently turns to alcohol for comfort, peace, relief, and fun, he or she has an alcoholic problem that affects you. In time, alcohol becomes his or her ultimate concern and saving grace. At that time, alcohol will displace even you and God in the problem drinker's life. No wonder you feel left out!

Unlike healthy people, alcoholics look forward to drinking, think about and give reasons for drinking, lie about and hide their drinking, or justify it. They feel a relentless urge to drink—to feel freer, to forget, to relax, to reward and nourish themselves, to feel better. The thought of *not* being able to drink for an indefinite time evokes anxiety and subtle sadness.

Remember that alcohol is a *drug*. It acts on and changes your brain chemistry. Initially, alcohol stimulates the pleasure center of the brain and gives us a high as well as reduces stress. Such effects are strong motives to drink again.

Alcoholics feel that they are *entitled* to drink and that life without alcohol is somehow not right, is incomplete, or is difficult. Although many alcoholics can abstain from drinking, they miss it. They may make efforts to abstain through sheer will power (the "white knuckle approach"). However, their "great sacrifice" reveals that, though they may be dry for the moment, the problem remains. Though abstinent, they become increasingly irritable, constantly complain, or even brag about their success in avoiding alcohol.

Remember: Your loved one's primary love is alcohol. Although your loved one probably loves you, when he or she is troubled or in need, they are more likely to go to the bottle than to you. Alcohol, not people and God, is their primary source of both comfort and consolation.

For this reason, alcoholic drinking impedes the healthiest and holiest experience—love for and from God, self, and others. Excessive drinking displaces God, alienates us from one another, and causes serious and unnecessary physical, psychological, and spiritual harm. Simply stated, excessive drinkers are people whose consumption of alcohol causes frequent and harmful problems to themselves and others. Their drinking causes more negative consequences than positive ones. Although the label "alcoholic" may not fit or may feel inappropriate, those who are obsessed with and compelled to use alcohol in spite of the negative consequences that outweigh the so-called positive ones are in fact alcoholics.

"WHY DO THEY DRINK SO MUCH?"

Why does the one you love drink so much? Nobody knows exactly why some people drink excessively. There are many theories about, and constant research to discover, the reasons people have problems with alcohol. Some scientists focus on genetic and biological factors such as biochemistry, genetic inheritance, brain functioning, and other biological factors. Others explore social factors like alcoholic modeling, social expectations, reinforcement, and marketing. Still others analyze psychological dynamics like habit formation, oral fixation, cognitive distortions, low self-esteem, poor coping skills, or emotional numbing. Spiritually, we can look at excessive drinking as a displacement of God. Instead of one cause, there is probably a tangled-up web of causality.

Fortunately, we do not need to know the cause(s) of alcoholism in order to make a difference. However, we do need to acknowledge what is going on, and then respond effectively. We can learn to diminish its effect on us, stop facilitating it, learn to manage it, and improve the quality of our lives.

FUNCTIONAL ALCOHOLISM

In light of our general discussion of alcoholism, let us look more specifically at functional alcoholism. One of the difficulties for both the drinker and yourself is that functional alcoholics are both "normal" and alcoholic. What this means is that functional alcoholics are normal insofar as they satisfy their needs, manage and cope effectively, communicate and work well, and behave within societal norms. At the same time, they drink alcoholically because they are obsessed with and compelled to use alcohol and because the negative consequences of their drinking are greater than the positive ones. Although they are more normal ("like us") than abnormal ("like them"), they are alcoholic and therefore not healthy.

Nevertheless, most functional alcoholics are not physically dependent on alcohol, but their affair with alcohol is more subtle, smoother, and secret. Functional or dysfunctional, *all* alcoholics are infatuated with alcohol.

Listen to Damian, a recovering functional alcoholic:

"It's not as if I was always thinking of drinking. I had to concentrate on my work as well. Actually, I was and am an excellent academic dean. However, to be honest, I looked forward to drinking after work. Drinking was my reward for a job well done; it motivated me.

"When I got home, my wife, kids, dogs, and a very dry double martini always greeted me. After the second double silver bullet, Jan, Bobby, Suzy, Pepper, and Salt became less important. I loved my family, but when push came to shove, alcohol was my main reward and source of comfort. A life without alcohol felt unfair, empty, and scary."

Most functional alcoholics eventually progress in their disease. However, it often takes them many years or decades to become relatively dysfunctional, powerless, and overtly disruptive. If there is a slow progression, both you and the alcoholic can more easily deny and enable the alcoholism. Furthermore, functional alcoholics often have periods of abstinence. For instance, "religious" alcoholics may quit during Lent only to resume on Easter. Some functional alcoholics abstain for months or even years and then return to drinking. Remember that being dry is *not* the same as being sober.

Because functional alcoholism is more normal than abnormal, your loved ones, and perhaps yourself, will probably have difficulty admitting to their alcoholism. The following questions may help you reflect on your loved one's drinking:

1. Does your loved one feel good about controlling his or her drinking?
2. Do you feel he is a better or nicer person when he is not drinking?
3. Does he miss drinking when he quits for a while?
4. Does he brag about never having caused or gotten into trouble because of his drinking?

5. Does he act or talk differently when drinking?
6. Is it difficult to have fun without drinking?
7. Is it a sacrifice for him to abstain from drinking at celebrations?
8. Does he feel more comfortable when drinking?
9. Does he have hangovers?
10. Do you think he might have a drinking problem or that he drinks too much?
11. Does he sometimes stop drinking?
12. Are many of his friends drinkers?
13. Does he drink secretively?
14. Does he justify his drinking?
15. Does his drinking cause more harm than good to him, you, and others?
16. Does his drinking impede communication?
17. Does his drinking impede intimacy?
18. Do you feel frustrated or angry when he drinks?
19. Do you feel alone and lonely when he drinks?
20. Do you feel tired, stuck, and discouraged?

A yes response to more than one of these questions should be a matter of concern; more than three positive responses indicate alcoholic drinking; and if you agree with more than six of these questions, your loved one is probably an alcoholic. If you have any doubt about his or her drinking, it behooves you to share your concern with an expert and/or a recovering alcoholic.

A caveat is that instead of centering on ourselves, we can become obsessed with the drinker. This, too, can cause serious trouble. In the next chapter, we will take a closer look at how to order our own lives in relation to the problem drinker.

Chapter Three

"How Can I Help?"

"Was it yesterday or a thousand years ago that I felt so numb and hopeless? I thought I had tried everything to get my husband to stop drinking—I reasoned, begged, screamed, threatened, pouted, cried, withdrew, collapsed. It seemed the more I did, the worse matters got. Nothing worked.

"I was also sick and weary from hiding, covering, lying, making excuses, putting up a front. Therefore, I shared my story with a friend at work. I chose this woman because she too was married to a wonderful person who drank too much. Yet she seemed spirited, serene, and generally happy. What was her secret?

"Well, in short, Laura introduced me to Al-Anon—a 12-step fellowship made for people like me. I listened to their stories—some worse than and some similar to mine. They shared what made things worse and better for them. I learned from listening, reading, thinking, sharing, and praying.

"I learned many things, especially that I couldn't change anyone except myself—and that exception made all the difference in the world. Although it may sound easy, it wasn't. It took a fair amount of time before I could really accept and act on this obvious fact.

"With the help of its members and my sponsor, I worked the program, sometimes with blind trust. I learned to love more effectively, to detach with compassion, to nurture and empower myself, to surrender to a Higher Power. I came to understand the insidious and sad nature of functional alcoholism as well as the insanity of my co-alcoholism. I came to realize that recovering from my codependency is the best gift I can give to myself and loved ones."

Although we cannot fix or make the drinker sober, we do have the power to change ourselves. Let us consider some things that we can do that will put us in a better position to help our loved ones—and ourselves.

We begin with ourselves, with recognizing and accepting our own faults. First, we search for the ways that we have unknowingly contributed to the drinking situation. When we can honestly look at and improve ourselves, we will help both our loved ones and ourselves. This is not as easy as it may sound, for many of us initially scrutinize the other instead of ourselves.

The following questions may give you some insight into this process of self-discernment. More than a couple of affirmative answers are good news: It means you can change your state of affairs.

1. Does your serenity depend too much upon your loved ones' attitude and behavior?
2. Does your mood vary with their drinking? When they drink, do you feel bad, and when they abstain, do you feel good?
3. Do you worry about how much they will drink?
4. Do you think too much about their drinking?
5. Do you frequently check up on your loved ones and feel responsible for them?
6. Do you think you know what is best for your loved ones?
7. Do you focus more on family members (spouse, child, parent, sibling, and friend) than on yourself? Do you think more about their needs, wants, and desires than your own?
8. Does your life center on the problem drinker?
9. Are you afraid to upset the drinker for fear it will set off a drinking bout?
10. Are you glad when holidays and celebrations are over, because of the drinking?
11. Are you out of touch with yourself, not knowing how you truly feel?
12. Do you frequently feel frustrated, angry, afraid, depressed, lonely, exhausted, disillusioned?

13. Are you becoming the person that you do not want to be?
14. Does it feel like the more you do, the worse things get?
15. Are you putting yourself aside and not taking care of yourself? Do you care for others more than you care for yourself?
16. Are you too tired too often?
17. Are you on edge even when you should be having fun?
18. Do you harbor resentment?
19. Do you sell yourself short and fail to recognize your accomplishments?
20. Does the quality of your life depend on the quality of the drinker's life?
21. Do you make the drinker more important than yourself?
22. Do you try to manage without God?
23. Do you blame God for what is happening?
24. Do you forget that God cares for and will help both you and your loved ones?
25. Do you wonder where God is?

We could go on and on, but you probably get the message. Part of the difficulty that is facing you is a result of focusing too much on the drinker and forgetting about yourself. The situation naturally worsens when we fail to focus on ourselves.

When you *need* someone you love to stop drinking and become sober, your life becomes centered on that person. In a sense, you make that person God insofar as you believe his or her sobriety will make you happy or save you from a miserable life. Theoretically we know better, but experientially this is the way we act. Most people who love a drinker think, feel, and act this way. In a sense, this is good because you are not alone, and you can do something about it.

BREAKING FREE FROM "ALCOHOL ENMESHMENT"

Listen to Pat who managed to break free from an alcohol trap:

"It was hell. I couldn't stop thinking about Jim's drinking. I kept thinking of ways to get Jim back to the person I fell in love with. I begged, argued, threatened, bribed, bargained, harangued, catered, reasoned, submitted, withdrew, loved, hated, and avoided to get him to change. You name it; I did it.

"But things only got worse. To compound matters, it seemed that he was the happy camper, and I was the miserable one. I used to say that I got the pain, and he got the gain. Something was terribly wrong, and I sensed that I had a hand in the mess.

"Only God knows why I didn't go crazy. Somehow, I came to realize that I was fighting a losing battle. With the help of God and a couple of friends, I began to let go of trying to change what was beyond my control—my husband. Instead of putting my happiness in Jim's hands, I learned to take responsibility for my own well-being.

"When I shifted my focus from my husband on to me, I initially felt selfish. Although it didn't feel right, it *was* right. After all, the only person I can change is myself. And you know what? When I became disentangled from Jim and sought more reliable sources of serenity, I learned to feel free and at peace regardless of what Jim did.

"I stopped looking at Jim as my saving grace—as God. It may sound corny, but it's true. When I turned to God and sober people, I ascended from hell and began to discover heaven on earth. And guess what? Jim began to seek help."

As long as your life is consumed with the drinker (which is not unlike the drinker being consumed with alcohol), life will get worse. To break out of the prison of alcohol enmeshment, you must focus on yourself and your relationship with God and others. With the help of God and others, we can begin to look differently at our loved ones and ourselves. This will be the catalyst we need for renewal.

Chapter Four

DANGEROUS BELIEFS AND EXPECTATIONS

In a psychology of addictions class, I ask the students if they can change people. With rare exceptions, they say no. Then I ask them if they try to change others. Invariably, they respond in unison: yes!

"Hmm," I say. "There seems to be a bit of a contradiction. Cognitive dissonance? Incongruence? Conflict? Discordance? Unbalance?" Then I explain that when we are aware of our disharmony, we can begin to listen, think, discuss, learn, and change.

Many of us hold and follow beliefs that contradict our conscious ones, particularly in times of stress. When we love a person who drinks too much, we often follow beliefs that we hold from the neck down, not those in our heads.

For instance: although we *know* that we cannot change the person we love, that does not stop us from persisting to do the impossible, or expect that person to change because of what we do. Clearly, there are reasons why life gets worse, and we feel miserable.

There are many reasons why we continue to try to change the person we love. We may simply want the drinker to feel and act better, or we may be afraid of the harm done to others, like children. Although our *intentions* are good, our *care* is misguided and ineffective. Actually, we will probably make things worse!

The most basic and frequent reason is that we need the drinker to change in order to feel better ourselves. When the satisfaction of our needs depends primarily on any "one" person, we court disaster. When *I* need *you* to be sober, or to listen to, respect, or love me, then I am in serious trouble. To be sure, *all* of us need love, affirmation, and respect. We need overall to be treated with goodness. However, when I need a *particular* person, like the drinker, to treat me well, I am placing my well-being in his or her hands as well as empowering them.

Although it is very challenging to change old habits, we can learn new ways that work better. Many begin with observing and listening to those who have achieved serenity in situations like their own. Particularly in the early stages of recovery, we have to trust the experience of others who have learned to change for the better. Initially, we often have to act contrary to our feelings and impulses, and have practically blind trust in those who have been successful. In a sense, we have to "fake it in order to make it," because we know it to be a better way. Eventually, what we know in our minds will be in our hearts.

SHOPPING FOR BREAD AT THE HARDWARE STORE?

Keep in mind that the drinker whom we love may be unwilling or incapable of giving us what we need. To *want* love from the drinker is fine; to *need* his or her love is disastrous.

It's like going to the hardware store to buy a loaf of bread. Looking oddly at you, the clerk (the drinker) offers you nails instead of bread. After all, he cannot give you what you need. In addition, as long as you insist that he satisfy your hunger (for sobriety), you will become increasingly dismayed, frustrated, angry, or simply exhausted. You might then respond in several ways, each of which changes your role. So you might—

- try to bribe the clerk or work a deal (and become a bargainer)
- try to manipulate the clerk by being very affirmative and obsequious (and become a pleaser)
- threaten and intimidate the clerk (and become the aggressor)
- simply leave the store in a huff (become a passive aggressor)

Whatever you do, the clerk *cannot* give you what you need or demand. The best way, of course, is to *accept* that hardware stores (functional alcoholics) do not stock bread (sobriety), and so instead go to a bakery or grocery store (healthy people and God).

Similarly, when it comes to meeting our own needs for love and security, we must not look to someone who is unable to fill those needs. On the contrary, we must learn to find ways to nourish ourselves, regardless of what our loved ones do. This involves reaching out to reliable people and turning to God. Out of this power basis, you will then be able to accept, cope with, and help the drinker—and, regardless of what the drinker does, *you can feel better and be happier*.

How do we get into such quicksand, needing and demanding what a person is unwilling or unable to give? There are many possible reasons.

For instance, some people come from a codependent background, and learned to pattern their behavior after someone who did not have a healthy sense of personal boundaries. They were taught to be responsible for the happiness of others. Trying to make another happy is especially futile when the other has serious problems, like a functional alcoholic has. These caretakers learned to believe that they have more power than they actually do. Other people never quite leave childhood in that they look outside themselves for happiness. Still others have a deep-seated and inappropriate need to serve others. Whatever the reasons, we lose perspective and forget how to care for ourselves. Let us look at some of the "blaming games" and other false assumptions that exacerbate our problems.

COMMON MISCONCEPTIONS

Parents are to blame if a child strays. One common misconception is to assume that if children are in trouble, parents are necessarily at fault. This is not always true. There are incorrigible children who come from the best homes, and children who come from the worst situations who become model adults.

Personal development is an extremely complex process, including innumerable factors from both nature and nurture. To be sure, parents play a major role in their children's formation, but parents do not have as much influence as they once had, when life was simpler and more homogenous.

I did something to cause the drinking problem. Another common mistake is to blame yourself (or others) for your loved one's problems. Actually, when you do this, you imply that you have more power than you actually have. It is as if you are saying that you could have controlled your loved one, or that his or her well-being was in your hands.

Yes, it is true that improving yourself will help make your situation more bearable for yourself. However, you do *not* have the power to manipulate others for the better. You did not cause the drinking, you cannot control it, and you cannot change or cure it. Conversely, when we admit to our individual (ego) powerlessness and surrender to a Higher Power, we will acquire more (spiritual) power.

If my loved one quits drinking, everything will be fine. This is another common but false belief, and it is dangerous for many reasons. Lasting happiness comes from three kinds of healthy relationships: with God, with yourself, and with other people. The drinker is just one part of that triad. Furthermore, it is a mistake to equate *abstinence* with *sobriety*. Some alcoholics become worse when they stop drinking because they are unable to deal with emergent issues that were once submerged in alcohol. *Sobriety* means that an alcoholic must learn to deal with his problems and effectively change his life.

Even if your loved one *does* become sober, life's inevitable problems, unfairness, and unhappiness will still occur. However, when we remove alcohol from the equation, we become better at coping with and growing from life's unpleasant and terrible vicissitudes. So it is imperative to be honest with yourself. Do you *need* the drinker to change for you to be happy? If so, you are compelled to achieve the impossible, programmed to make life worse, and sentenced to life misery. If you feel you *must* change the drinker, you will become the other side of the drinking coin, becoming very similar to what you detest: instead of being dependent on alcohol, you are *dependent* on the alcoholic, or, you are *co*dependent. This is a common mistake: putting your well-being in the hands of an incompetent person.

When we act on false beliefs, we lose our vital balance. In trying to make the impossible happen, we fail to satisfy our needs, and we become increasingly more frustrated and upset. Like the drinker, we look outside ourselves and fail to see and connect with the source of equanimity dwelling within us.

Our challenge is to avoid mistaken and dark ways, and to seek and follow the way of truth and light. With help, we humbly admit our mistaken beliefs, and eventually we "learn to unlearn" old ways that impede growth. We can learn new ways to see and act effectively. We can connect with the human-and-divine abiding within and beyond us. Such transcendent bonding enables us to attain abiding security, safety, satisfaction, and serenity.

Similar to false beliefs, unrealistic and inflexible expectations can also add to a troublesome situation. This is especially true when our sense of well-being is dependent upon our loved one's ability to meet those expectations.

Of course, all people have some kind of expectations about what will satisfy their needs and make them feel good. For example, if someone offers you a free week in Aruba, you expect that you are going to have a great time—and chances are, you probably will. On the other hand, if we have expectations about someone who is unable to give us what we need, we quickly become unsatisfied and unhappy. Returning to the vacation example, if you have every day of your trip planned out in advance, only to have it rain on your parade, if you are not sufficiently flexible, your vacation will be ruined. Likewise, if you have expectations about the drinker that he or she is unable to meet, you are going to wind up, at best, disappointed.

There is usually a negative correlation between expectations and serenity: the greater our expectations, the less serenity we feel. If you need your unrealistic expectations to be fulfilled, you are going to be miserable.

When you expect a drinker to be reliable and responsible, you are asking for trouble. When you refuse to deviate from your expectations because you need the drinker to respond a certain way, you are setting yourself up to be frustrated. When you expect the drinker to listen to and understand your honest sharing, eventually you will become frustrated, hurt, and probably angry. When you expect the drinker to be grateful for your generosity, you will sooner than later be let down.

WATCH OUT FOR PIGEONS

When dealing with a drinker, it is prudent to have very flexible expectations, and also to have plans B, C, and D, just in case plan A is thwarted. For example, when a woman expects her husband to take their son to a ballgame on a night when he usually drinks, her alternative plans could include her or another responsible person taking her son to the game. Instead of making excuses for her husband, she could let him take the consequences of his behavior, and gently tell her son that daddy is drinking again. Thus, she avoids enabling her husband while enabling her son to have a good time.

When living with a functional alcoholic, you have to be ready for anything. Having highly flexible expectations will lessen your frustration and increase your coping skills. You simply cannot let your well-being depend on the drinker fulfilling your expectations.

To illustrate, I am reminded of a story about two people who worked together for a certain charity. After working a long shift, they took a walk outside and stopped to rest on a park bench. As they sat, one of them felt something fall into her hair. She looked up and was splattered with pigeon poop.

Immediately, she stood up and shouted at the pigeon and at God, "God, I've given my life to you and to help your people, and this is what I get: crapped on."

Turning around, she saw that her friend had moved to another bench and that she was smiling and almost chuckling.

"Stop laughing! Just what is so funny anyway?" the first woman demanded.

Her friend simply smiled and said, "What are you so upset about? That's what pigeons do."

If we expect pigeons not to do what pigeons do—that is, if we expect alcoholics to behave otherwise—we base our expectations on false beliefs. We can blame the drinker, the alcohol, God, or anyone else, but problem drinkers will do what problem drinkers do—they cause disruption. Know that alcoholics more or less think, feel, choose, and act differently than healthy people. To assume and expect otherwise is a prescription for misery. So long as we do not accept this fact, we will find ourselves up to our necks in pigeon poop.

Only our Higher Power is always there for us. God is the only one we can depend upon with certitude. Indeed, even God does not meet all our expectations, for they may not be good for us. We can trust God to know what is best for us and to provide the power and grace to cope with problems with serenity.

As long as we obsess about the drinker (which is not unlike the drinker who obsesses about alcohol), life will get worse. To break out of the prison of alcoholic enmeshment, we must focus on ourselves and our relationship with God and others. With their help, we can begin to look differently at our loved ones and ourselves. This will be the catalyst we need for renewal.

Chapter Five

MORE WELL-INTENTIONED MISTAKES

We have seen that acting on our false beliefs about our loved one's drinking is like trying to put out a fire with gasoline. We unknowingly use fuel instead of water, expect to extinguish the fire, and become baffled when the fire increases.

Be assured: You did not start the fire by making your loved one drink. Unless you physically pour alcohol down his or her throat, you cannot make another drink alcoholically. However, your response to another person's drinking can "fuel the fire," enabling the problem to flare up even worse than before. On the other hand, if you avoid ineffective coping methods, the fire is more likely to remain manageable, and you are unlikely to get burned. Refusing to fuel the fire of alcoholism will also help the drinker to quench it.

It is normal to protect yourself when you feel hurt, afraid, confused, guilty, or ashamed. And yet sometimes the ways we cope are not only ineffective but ultimately harmful. We will address a number of these negative coping mechanisms later in the chapter. For now, we will look at the two most common ways to ward off anxiety that results from unacceptable feelings: denial and repression.

DENIAL AND REPRESSION

A defense prevalent with both alcoholics and those who love them is *denial*. Denial occurs when we refuse or are unable to admit what is obvious to many and especially to the trained eye. For instance, you are in denial when your loved one is withdrawn, oppositional, or mellow, and you are unable to link it with alcohol. You do not recognize the sarcasm, seductive words, or silence as a manifestation of alcohol consumption.

Why would anyone use such an ineffective way to deal with a painfully obvious reality? Why expunge experiences from conscious awareness? Usually, it is because we have learned and relearned that certain experiences are "unacceptable." They make no sense, are bad in themselves, and are something that "no good person" would experience.

Some of us learned early in life that to maintain self-esteem or to feel "lovable," we had to deny certain realities. To admit them, and often the anger and fear associated with them, would cause us to risk rejection or evoke unhealthy guilt (self-rejection).

Adults usually begin to learn these behaviors in childhood. If a girl's alcoholic parents, for example, constantly deny behaviors and repress feelings associated with drinking, as well as punish any awareness and verbalization about drinking, the child learns that her self-esteem depends on denying alcoholic behavior and repressing consequent feelings. Although her denial and repression satisfy her parents, foster collusion, and maintain shaky esteem, she violates herself and enables her parents to drink. When the truth demands recognition, she is apt to change the subject, argue the point, rationalize the alcoholic behavior, or just withdraw in silence. All these behaviors fuel the fire of alcoholism.

As this child grows to womanhood, she does not realize that her anxious feelings are linked to drinking and its dire consequences. She may have little idea why she is unhappy. Because she never learned to listen to her anxious and fearful self, her denial and repression seriously impede healthy communication. This woman carries the heavy and exhausting burden of feeling forbidden to feel, trust, or speak the truth. With good but fatal intentions, she fuels the fire of alcoholic collusion and perpetuates the damage.

Although we may achieve some short-term gains with such negative coping, like some semblance of love and reduction of pain, our long-term losses are much greater and debilitating. Negative defenses impede both the drinker's recovery and the personal growth of those who love him or her. And so, it is wise to break out of these defenses, for they distort your perception of reality. Moreover, they cause you to waste much time and energy in repetitive behavior that only makes things worse.

Those who fixate in denial remain silent, not talking to themselves, others, the alcoholic, or even God about the nature of the problem. And as long as we are in denial, things get worse and recovery is practically impossible. Instead, we continue to fuel and stoke the fire of alcoholic drinking and wonder why we continue to get burned.

To compound our distortions, denial will often include more than one person. Such *collusion* means that two or more people, without consciously agreeing, deny the same reality. Frequently, we join the drinker's denial, entering a covert contract of mutual pretense. The script goes something like this:

- I'll pretend that you do not drink too much,
- if you pretend that I am not pretending,
- and we'll both pretend that life is all right.

Everyone acts as if an elephant (the drinker) is not in the middle of the living room. More importantly, everyone thinks they manage to avoid the elephant poop (the consequences). For example, it is common for parents to deny their son's or daughter's drinking, or for the laity to deny obvious evidence of a cleric's drinking. So long as everyone is deaf and blind, alcohol problems escalate.

When things get worse, you may even find yourself stretching the truth or simply lying about your loved one's behavior:

- You may tell his or her boss or others that he has a cold rather than a hangover.
- You may help him avoid people and thus never invite anyone to your house.
- You may make excuses for his shy or boisterous behavior.
- You lie, rather than tell the truth in a compassionate way.

Understandably, you may be ashamed to admit that your loved one drinks too much. Yet, covering the truth facilitates the very behavior that you detest. It usually is better to avoid taking responsibility for the drinker. Rather than making excuses or covering up, you can step out of the way and let your loved ones take responsibility for their own behavior.

Repression, like denial, is an unconscious effort to exclude certain experiences from conscious awareness. We deceive ourselves by pushing certain realities out of conscious recall and by not admitting our feelings about certain events. Although we may feel frustrated and angry, we pretend not to be. Confusing? Yes.

When we repeatedly repress our feelings, we live in a world of make-believe. When you repress your feelings about problem drinking, you do not consciously choose to lie to yourself. Repression, like most negative coping, is primarily an unconscious process. Although you may feel anxious about your feelings centered on drinking, you cannot allow yourself to reflect on them.

If someone confronts you about your feelings, you will probably feel threatened and consequently become even more defensive. To avoid the truth, you may innocently deny it, anxiously withdraw from it, vehemently protest it, or sincerely intellectualize it. It is very difficult to accept that your loved one is an alcoholic, albeit a functional one.

When we are afraid and hurting, denial and repression are more likely to occur than honest acceptance. It is painful to face and effectively deal with the difficulties and lost dreams of alcoholic drinking. Understandably, our anxiety can motivate us to employ even more defenses that initially protect but eventually harm ourselves and abet the drinker.

OTHER HARMFUL DEFENSES

Rationalization

Rationalization is an irrational way of using rationality. We rationalize when we explain and justify behavior and feelings associated with alcohol with socially acceptable reasons. Examples include:

- "Almost everyone drinks!"
- "Well, he doesn't always drink."

- "She works hard and deserves to unwind with a drink if she wants to."
- "He pays the bills, and should be able to have a few beers if he wants."
- "Most men drink—and some of them a lot more than he does!"

Rather than facing the scary situation, we make excuses, cover up, or justify it.

Minimization

Minimizing a person's drinking and its consequences is another common reaction. You can find yourself saying things like:

- "Sometimes he drinks too much, but he is not a drunk."
- "She may drink too much, but after all she is a home-maker and has a career."
- "He couldn't have a drinking problem; he's never even gotten in trouble."
- "He deserves to have some fun."
- "Compared to others, he doesn't drink a lot."

In short, your distorted perception of your loved one's drinking enables the drinker to drink even more and you to feel more miserable.

Catastrophic Thinking

Some of us are prone to obsessing about the worst possible result of our loved one's drinking—maximizing the negative and minimizing the positive. When this happens, our negative vision only engenders more anxiety and fear, and further distorts our perception. Consequently, we are less able to manage effectively. If we are perfectionists, we are especially prone to catastrophic thinking: if we cannot have 100 percent, we settle for 0 percent. Literally, all or nothing.

The danger of assuming the worst outcome is that we can feel overwhelmed, helpless, and hopeless. For instance, if your drinking teenager is out long past her curfew, you think the worst rather than remaining patient and open to what eventually unfolds.

"Life will never get better"… "I am doomed to a miserable life"…"The children will be failures"…"Nobody loves me"…"If only he would die"—all these are the laments of the catastrophic enabler. Such "catastrophizing" drains and weakens us.

Worry and catastrophizing seek each other as destructive dance partners. When we worry, we obsess about the negative things that might happen. The worst possible scenarios plague our minds, drain our energy, and decrease our freedom to act appropriately. Although we care when we worry, we are also trying to control the future according to our will. Worry is well intentioned, but it is futile, makes matters worse, and is a waste of time and energy. You can learn better ways to care.

Emotional Blunting

Emotional blunting is the result of protecting yourself against the hurt and disappointment of drinking by restricting emotional expression and vulnerability. Being warm and approachable is too painful, so you keep cool and distant. For example, if your daughter is in trouble, you might remain distant and intellectualize about a passing phase of development rather than getting involved and seeking the truth. Or if your spouse is manipulative and abusive, you may hide behind an impenetrable glass wall that protects (and suffocates) you. Yet, such emotional restriction and detachment may be temporarily necessary in order to survive with the hope of someday thriving.

Listen to this woman whose husband refuses to admit that his son is drinking alcoholically:

"My husband, Dave, feels powerless to help our son, and he feels guilty when he gets angry. So, he shuts up and makes himself unavailable. Dave gets very detached and cold, especially when I ask him how he really feels about our son. He won't even join a support group. He says that he can handle it on his own."

Whatever the reason, Dave has probably learned to cope with his uncomfortable feelings by being *too* detached and insulated. It is sad because he cares, but his coping impedes his caring and alienates his wife.

Insulation and Isolation

Similarly, *insulation* and *isolation* occur when a person cuts himself off from situations that produce stress. To withdraw freely from a situation can be healthy, but to be compelled to withdraw from any situation that involves drinking is not healthy. Dave in our previous example both insulates and isolates.

Or, consider a woman (or man) who isolates herself in her bedroom when her husband drinks. Rather than facing her alienation, she represses her feelings and isolates herself, while protecting herself from the painful truth. She may even use drugs to numb, insulate, and isolate herself even more. In cruel irony, she *increases* the very feelings she wants to lessen.

Projection

Projection involves blaming others for our own unacceptable feelings, and is another way to compound the problem of drinking. For example, you may blame the problem drinker for your unhappiness. You say, "If he would only stop drinking, then I would be happy," or "If my spouse had been stricter (or more lenient), our child would not be drinking."

When we blame others, we abdicate responsibility and place our well-being in the hands of the alcoholic rather than in our own. We falsely and fatally assume that our happiness depends on the alcoholic becoming sober. Besides, it is unfair and stressful to the alcoholic, which once again puts more fuel on the fire of alcoholism.

ALTERNATIVES TO CONSIDER

At some point, our defenses weaken and may even break down, and the painful truth will demand to be heard. Some prevent this breakdown by holding on tightly to their defenses. Others numb their pain with drugs. Yet, some *do* break through to liberating truth. The sooner you become aware of your feelings and the reality they point to, the better off you are. You not only circumvent pain for yourself, but you stop enabling the drinker. Of course, *how* we express our feelings is important.

To express anger at a drinker may be honest, but it seldom solves anything and usually worsens matters. Although the blunt expression of anger may give temporary relief, it is likely to increase your anger and not resolve the issue. Anger tends to alienate and hurt. Both repression and crass expression usually exacerbate the situation.

A healthier approach is to listen to your angry feelings and reflect on appropriate ways to respond to their message. Remember that *anger* is usually a secondary feeling that covers other primary feelings like frustration, fear, and hurt. Our challenge is to understand and attend to these underlying feelings.

Indeed, it is a rare person who can be aware of, accept, and act appropriately in the early stages of a loved one's drinking. The more common approach is to be unaware of our feelings and assumptions and to react in ways that exacerbate alcoholic drinking. Since this is an unconscious process, how do you become aware of what is happening?

Some people come to accept reality when their pain becomes too great; others remain in perpetual denial. When the truth is less painful than our negative coping, we are apt to admit to what is going on. Then we can begin to learn effective ways of coping and helping. Unfortunately, many of us have to break *down* and bottom out in order to break *through*.

However, this does not *always* have to happen. You can pause, listen to, and think about what someone might say about your loved one's drinking. Rather than passing off their feedback as an overreaction, give it a second thought.

With problem drinking (and life in general), pray for the grace to be open, honest, and willing to listen and change. For most people, it takes time for their feelings to gradually work their way to conscious awareness so they can be named, claimed, and managed. So long as you do not accept that your loved one is an alcoholic and that you are a co-alcoholic, it is unlikely that either you or your loved one can be helped. The saving paradox, however, is that nonacceptance is the usual road to acceptance—the gateway to positive change.

Chapter Six

ENABLING

We have seen that even with the best intentions, we can behave in ways that foster the opposite of what we want to achieve. Understandably, you can become baffled and frustrated about how things get worse when you are trying so hard to make them better. We have emphasized the importance of becoming aware of how our well-intentioned behavior facilitates the drinking and empowers the drinker.

Listen to this woman:

"It took me a long time to realize that the more I did, the worse things got. My primary goal in life was to get Fred to stop drinking. Mind you, Fred was not a drunk. He was a good worker, and a decent father and husband too, I guess. So, why wasn't I satisfied?

"One of my sources of irritation was that after dinner Fred would start drinking. He would never get roaring drunk, but he would have two or three stiff martinis, soon fade away, and finally fall asleep by 10 o'clock or earlier. It was as if he was in his own world and out of ours. Indeed, our life suffered and the kids got shortchanged.

"Take vacations, for example. For Fred, a vacation without drinking was no vacation at all. Fred would start drinking about four or five in the afternoon and by early evening he'd get that stupid grin on his face. I wasn't sure I could trust him when we went out in the evening. I always felt insecure. Although he never got into trouble, he always seemed to be on the edge.

"When the kids got older, I joined him in vacation drinking for a few years. We had some alcoholic fun, but we always seemed to meet in a fog. Dialogues were more like separate monologues. Sex was sex, not much open love. Nevertheless, I tried to satisfy his needs. I was always on call.

"Indeed, I tried everything throughout our twenty-two-year marriage. I did everything Fred would ask. I kind of assumed that if I would be the perfect wife, he would see the light and stop drinking. If I loved him enough, I reasoned, he would stop. For a long time, I would buy his favorite booze, make excuses for his absence, kept his drinking secret. After all, he was a well-known and well-liked man of the community. If only I would do better, maybe he would be better. What a jerk.

"I eventually became frustrated and angry, and began to confront him. He would counter that he was not an alcoholic as evidenced by his perfect work attendance. He never got into trouble, and he was an active member in the community and church. He always seemed to win the arguments.

"Finally, I got exhausted and gave up. I simply withdrew and avoided the whole matter. I became a married celibate. I tried everything. What should I do?"

WHAT IS AN ENABLER?

You may identify with this woman, for she describes a classic and common case of enabling. Enabling involves taking responsibility for the drinker and facilitating the drinking. We have already seen that acting on false beliefs and unrealistic expectations, as well as using negative defense mechanisms, can enable our loved one to drink. Consider some other common ways to enable.

Buying alcohol may seem to be a blatant example of enabling, but it is not as simple as it sounds. Remember, most alcoholics are quite functional, and alcohol pleases them. Thus, if you want to please your loved one, you buy alcohol. Invariably, his or her response is gratitude and appreciation, which initially feels good but eventually ends in frustration.

As enablers, we are prone to err by being overly responsible. Although we ought to be responsible *to* one another, with some exceptions, we should not be responsible *for* one another. Every time we take over the responsibility of our loved one, we avoid letting the drinker be responsible for himself. For instance, we clean the drinker after he has been sick, or we lie to his boss when he misses work.

Consistently accommodating or making excuses for the drinker is a form of enabling. To change your schedule, to miss or be late for an event, to make invalid excuses, to accept unacceptable behavior, or to have sex to please are forms of such enabling.

When your life centers on the drinker, you can easily find yourself compensating for and rationalizing a drinker's misbehavior. There is seldom a good reason to be responsible for or to compensate for a drinker's irresponsibility. As long as you make yourself responsible, he or she is less likely to change. To recover, drinkers must learn to be responsible. To be sure, there are exceptions, but they should be true exceptions. If the drinker's responsibility is to pay the utility bills, and he fails to do so, it may be wise to pay the bill yourself if the electricity or gas is going to be turned off. Overall, our goal is to let the drinker take the consequences of his or her drinking, but not to the detriment of ourselves and loved ones.

While caring for one another is part of being a family, helping the drinker to avoid the negative consequences of his or her actions is usually enabling and counterproductive. For instance, if a loved one occasionally falls asleep watching television, we might put a blanket on him. On the other hand, if this person usually has several drinks and falls asleep, thereby avoiding family interaction, the same action of covering actually encourages the behavior.

Similarly, people have difficulty recalling a particular word in conversation from time to time. However, if you frequently finish the alcoholic's sentences and remember details for him because he is drinking too much, you are enabling. The same is true when he gets a little out of line socially, and you make excuses and cover for him.

Rather than let him make a fool of himself, you rescue him. In time this becomes exhausting because you not only have to take care of yourself, you also have to be constantly alert and care for him. With reasonable exceptions, we should not bail out our loved ones or cover up for their behavior.

WHAT SHOULD A PARENT DO?

In regard to an adolescent or an adult child, abstaining from enabling can be especially difficult. Understandably, when our children get into trouble, we *want* to rescue them. And with many children, this is the most appropriate response. With alcoholics and other drug abusers, however, it is tempting to bail them out and consequently enable them. When we witness our child's present and future life crumble, we can easily make loving but wrong decisions.

Let the words of these parents resonate with you:

"It wasn't easy for us to let our seventeen-year-old son go to jail. The first time he was caught for drunk driving, he promised to mend his ways. So, we bailed him out, and for three months he didn't drink. We thought we did the right thing. Then, he started to drink again and quickly got busted for the same offense. And we rescued him again. It seemed that we were going around in circles, getting nowhere. The third time, with the support of a 12-step group, we let him stay in jail.

"We told him that we loved him and that he had to be responsible for the consequences of his behavior. He played on our guilt, saying that if we loved him, we wouldn't let him rot in jail. His grandparents also thought that we were mean and vindictive. Nevertheless, we kept our stand, and at the hearing we encouraged the judge to send our son to a treatment facility. It was the toughest and best thing we could have done for him.

"We didn't give up on him, and we never will. But we had to let go of our own old enabling ways and learn new ways to love. No matter what happens, we know that our son is in God's hands and that God will and does care for him."

These courageous and loving parents broke away from their previous enabling to let their son have the opportunity to learn from the consequences of his drinking. They came to realize that they could not save their son, and they learned a better way to help him. They put him in the hands of a Higher Power, believing that, with God, redemptive recovery would sooner or later occur.

CAN ENABLING EVER BE
A GOOD THING?

Sometimes negative enabling is unavoidable and may be the better albeit imperfect way to give our loved one an opportunity to improve his or her situation. For example, if you let your problem spouse, adult child, friend, or parent live with you, rather than make their own separate arrangements, you might then be enabling him or her to have more money to buy alcohol and to circumvent negative consequences. On the other hand, living with a drinker might give you the opportunity to be a role model, to intervene, or to respond in helpful ways. Sometimes, we have to decide whether the positive influence outweighs the negative one.

Thus, we can see that there are two kinds of enabling: positive and negative. *Positive enabling* means that we increase the likelihood of healthy behavior. Teachers, doctors, counselors, ministers, and many others are in the profession of enabling people to improve their lives. Parents, spouses, siblings, relatives, and friends can have a similar intent. When we are good role models, offer help, set boundaries, detach, and allow our loved ones to suffer the consequences of their drinking, we enable them to recover.

However, when we deny or rationalize their behavior, collude with them, become responsible for them, become enmeshed, or fail to allow them to suffer, we interfere with their becoming sober. *One of the highest measures of love is to let our loved ones hurt.* With good intentions, we are prone to ease their pain and consequently enable their alcoholic drinking and impede their recovery.

In short, although we cannot change anyone else, we *can* change ourselves, and therefore make a difference. In order to do that, we need to—

- adjust our unrealistic expectations and beliefs
- recognize and eliminate negative coping and enabling behaviors

- stop taking inappropriate responsibility
- allow our loved ones to suffer their consequences

Such loving behavior is difficult, but necessary and doable. Remember: this tough love is best for both you and your loved one.

Chapter Seven

PEOPLE PLEASERS AND OTHER TOXIC LOVES

When our well-being depends on and fluctuates according to our loved one's behavior, we will do almost anything to fix, enlighten, convert, and sober up him or her. Out of love and pain, we try to do the impossible—to change the drinker. Our challenge is to learn to care differently. To achieve this goal, let us look at additonal counterproductive ways we may be caring.

We have already discussed how our good intentions often lead to bad results. We sincerely try to help but end up enabling the drinker. We have also pointed out that recognizing this is actually a hopeful sign, because it indicates that there is something we *can* change: *ourselves*. When we stop enabling, we help *both* ourselves *and* our loved ones.

Why we care one way rather than another is due to a multiplicity of factors from nature and nurture, like temperament, past learning, family dynamics, role models, self-worth, and random chance. The key to improvement is to discover our ways of caring for our loved ones and how they can be improved.

PEOPLE PLEASERS

Many of us center our care on a hyperpropensity to please. We are willing to do anything for the one we love. We are always on call, ready to serve. Abhorring conflict and fights, we seek peace at the cost of our own rights and well-being. We are likely to take care of the drinker's negative consequences as well as make excuses for and minimize his disruptive behavior.

We rarely blame others for difficulties, but are likely to take and even *ask for* the blame ourselves. We always look for the fault within ourselves, assuming that if we can correct the fault, we can control, change, and correct the situation. Such thinking is common and false. As "12-steppers" would say, it is "stinkin' thinkin'."

Of course, if the drinker is a "blamer" and you are a "blamee," then you get into a pathetic relationship: He falsely blames you, and you plead guilty. He gives you a sentence, and you serve it. You falsely assume that if you take the blame you can correct your faults and things will improve. More likely, life gets worse.

People pleasing can be a form of *manipulation*. We may sincerely think that if we comply with all requests, our loved one will eventually come to his or her senses and get sober. "How could the drinker refuse a request from someone who is so good?" we may ask. Although we usually do not *consciously* intend to manipulate, our underlying motive is to change the person so that not only the drinker but we, too, feel better.

Our love is *conditional*, for when our loved one does not respond favorably to our good acts, we soon get hurt, bent out of shape, and angry. Our challenge is to learn to depend upon the Higher Power of unconditional Divine Love so that we will be less tempted to place our serenity into the hands of a troubled person.

PERFECTIONISTS

Similar to the people pleaser is the perfectionist. As perfectionists, we expect nothing less than perfection. Besides being irritated by the alcoholic's imperfect behavior, we expect ourselves to be perfect. We try to be the *perfect* listener, the *perfect* lover, the *perfect* servant, the *perfect* caretaker, the *perfect* spouse, and the *perfect* parent, assuming that if we are *perfect*, things will get better.

Again, this is a false belief and an unrealistic expectation. Even if we were perfect, which simply is impossible, our loved one would still drink. We are better off to accept with serenity the imperfections in ourselves and our loved one. After all, *love is for imperfect people*.

As pleasers and perfectionists, we need validation from the drinker. Making a drinker the source of our well-being, we make ourselves vulnerable to being manipulated. For instance, when your loved one smiles at or expresses gratitude for your "perfect" behavior, you are apt to feel good and to go along with his or her drinking. You will do almost anything to get him to like and to love you, even to enable him to drink. Thus, we get into a dance of manipulation: you manipulate the drinker, and the drinker manipulates you. Such a relationship is not as cold and calculating as it may sound, for our intentions are usually benevolent and desperate.

SERVERS, SAVIORS, AND MARTYRS

If you are a server, you feel perpetually "on call" to make things right. If the drinker is oppositional, you are kind; if he is withdrawn, you take initiative; if he forgets, you remember; if he is withdrawn, you get involved; if he is loud, you are silent; if he is quiet, you talk. Servers tend to be obsequious, deferring to the drinker's wishes. It is as if we are slaves in service of the drinker. We are on earth to do the will of the other—in this case, the drinker.

Saviors and martyrs believe that if they are good enough, or if they find the right love formula or latest therapeutic technique, the drinker will see the light. Again, at first listening, this may *sound* good. However, *the fact is that we cannot save anyone!* We can only give people the opportunity and show them the way. Even Jesus Christ did not make people change, make them good, or convert them against their will. Rather, Christ offered them the way, the truth, and the life to change. He invited them to use their reason to increase their faith in a Higher Power.

CONDITIONAL LOVE

Sometimes, because of past deficiencies, our need for affection and approval becomes so great that our world revolves around other people, including and especially the drinker, while we minimize ourselves and God. The wishes and opinions of our loved ones count more than our own and perhaps even God's. We make others bigger and stronger than they are, and ourselves smaller and weaker. Since we need others to love and appreciate us, we are vulnerable to a partner who will run our life. Consequently, we diminish our worth and God's grace.

Maybe you can feel for this forty-three year old woman:

> "I feel so ashamed of myself. For the past twenty years, I've participated in behavior that I would never tolerate in my children or condone for anyone. I've been a slave to my husband. I've taken verbal abuse, enabled his drinking, and even joined him in sexual activities that demean me and are against God's law.
>
> "Why? I guess I was afraid of losing him. Or, I thought that if I gave him what he wanted, he would stop drinking and become the man that he was or hoped he would become when I married him. You know, sometimes he would be nice, and I would melt and be ready to give, give, give. His five percent seemed to equal my 95 percent."

We may believe that love and being loved will make everything right. But this kind of "love" pressures us to please, serve, and collude, as well as to dread desertion and solitude. Our saving grace becomes the drinker rather than healthy relationships with God and others. We learn to be content with very little, to restrict ourselves inordinately, to be last in line, to sell ourselves terribly short. When a cookie tastes like a gourmet meal, we empower the drinker to control us by feeding us crumbs.

The more conditions we hold to, the more unnecessary suffering there will be. Conditions—like needing approval, love, and guidance, or needing the absence of disapproval, rejection, and avoidance—are common and decidedly human. However, when we look for such needs to be satisfied from someone who is unwilling or unable to do so, we make ourselves vulnerable to being manipulated as well as to manipulate.

As simple as it sounds, we must look to *healthy* love for our sustenance. When we place our well-being in loving hands, we are less likely to manipulate and be manipulated. Instead of looking outside ourselves for our well-being, we can look to God and to people of love. Instead of begging for rarely attainable love, we can seek the Source of Love, or our Higher Power. We can please and serve God who wants us to please and love ourselves. When we follow God's will—to love ourselves as well as, and not less than, others, and to place our well-being in God's love—we will come to experience freedom and serenity.

Chapter Eight

AGGRESSIVE AND AVOIDANT CARETAKERS

Not everyone responds to a problem drinker through accommodation or people pleasing. Some express their care aggressively and are more overt and blatant in trying to change things.

If we are aggressive caretakers, rather than moving *toward* our loved ones, we move *against* them. We operate out of a power base that tries to stop our loved ones from drinking through the use of force. We intimidate, threaten, and give ultimatums. Assuming that *we* know what is best for the drinker, we aggressively try to make the drinker get sober.

Although we love the drinker, we tend to underestimate and even disrespect his or her rights, dignity, feelings, and needs—in contrast to people pleasers, who overestimate them. If our loved one is also a hostile type, life becomes a war with many battlefronts. If our drinker is compliant, he or she may temporarily follow our orders but will soon return to drinking.

As aggressive caretakers, we act as if *we* are the truth and the way to a healthy life. However, unlike God, we try to *force* our loved ones to see our light, to face our truth, and to follow our way. When the drinker does not submit to our dictates, we become more frustrated and angry, and try to control even more. We aggressively use fuel to extinguish the fire of drinking, and then become furious when the fire escalates. Eventually, we burn out.

In reality, our will-to-power is often a cover and overcompensation for our own weakness. Our control protects us from being hurt and gives us the *illusion* of superiority. One of our challenges is to face our fears and humbly ask God to help us heal. Rather than trying to save and cure our loved ones, we can humbly admit that we have much less power over the drinker than we assume. Paradoxically, when we accept our powerlessness, we *enable ourselves* to discover a Higher Power.

AVOIDING THE PROBLEM?

Rather than moving toward or against problematic loved ones, some people simply avoid them altogether. We stay out of the way. Yet our self-sufficiency, independence, and unavailability not only harm ourselves but also enable the drinker. Like the pleaser, the *avoider* lets problem people get away with what they want.

There are many reasons for such manipulative love. For instance, we may want to hide from the alcoholic turmoil and the fear and hurt that go with it. Understandably, we want to insulate and protect ourselves through our detachment, assuming that, if we withdraw, nothing can hurt us. Or perhaps we are trying to retaliate by withholding cooperation and love, thereby "forcing" the drinker into sobriety. Rather than the tepidity of the pleaser or the heat of the aggressor, we use the passive-aggressive coldness of withdrawal.

By putting emotional distance between ourselves and the drinker, we rarely fight or argue like our aggressive brothers and sisters, nor do we cater to the drinker like our compliant brethren. Since we avoid emotional involvement, we minimize the pain of fights, rejections, manipulations, and disappointments. However, we risk the more insidious and lethal pain of indifference.

Still, it is not uncommon to withdraw from and avoid your loved one because you are frustrated and exhausted. After fueling the fire of alcoholism with aggression and compliance, you may feel that nothing will work, or that you need a well-deserved rest. You experience your powerlessness over the alcoholic, and, in a sense, you hit your own bottom.

Feeling fed up and even giving up may be your saving grace. Feeling numb and wanting nothing to do with your loved one may enable you to take care of yourself, gain new perspective, and learn to cope more effectively. Try not to feel guilty for feeling so good! Such a vacation from futility is often necessary, but vacations are temporary. The caveat is to *fixate in indifference*—the most dangerous enemy of love.

RELATIONSHIP STYLES

We have seen that over time each individual develops a certain style for caring and communicating, solving and coping with stress, and managing difficulties. This style develops from both *nature* (one's inherited predispositions and potential) and *nurture* (the environments in which that person develops).

When conflicts arise, more often than not the opposing sides subscribe to different coping styles. For instance, if you are compliant, then he or she is likely to be domineering or avoidant. Consequently, you engage in and foster a problematic relationship. But having the same style can also cause problems. Two hostile people will consistently fight; two compliant people will kill each other with kindness; two avoidant people will live alone and ultimately die alone.

All of these styles of caring contain truth, and they can be appropriate in moderation. To choose to please another or to comply with a reasonable request can be healthy. Sometimes, aggressive action is the best, although imperfect, way. Even avoidance may be a way to show love. But when any of these styles are taken to the extreme and aim to change or manipulate the drinker, we are out of bounds, and *we* need to change.

PARENTING STYLES

Parents are likely to have different styles of caring for a loved one, especially when a child is a substance abuser. For instance, you may be a pleaser, giving your child almost anything he or she wants in order to stop drinking. Meanwhile, your spouse may threaten, argue with, or overtly try to control your child. Or, Mom may be the dominator, while Dad withdraws into his own world.

It is common for an alcoholic child to play one parent against the other. For instance, the alcoholic is likely to deal more with the compliant parent and avoid or argue with the aggressive one. The aggressive parent can be made the bad guy and the pleasing parent the good guy. When such triangulation exists, the stability and health of both the marriage and the family are easily threatened. Indeed, the excessive drinking of *one* family member impacts *everyone*. *Alcoholism is a family disease.*

The most important thought to keep in mind, however, is that in order to help your loved ones, you must first help yourself. For example, when a plane has mechanical problems and the oxygen masks are disengaged, the prudent mother first puts the mask on herself and then on her child. The imprudent but equally caring mother puts the oxygen first on her daughter, and then passes out, unable to help her daughter later on.

In the same way, if you take care of your own needs so that you are strengthened to love effectively, you are in much better shape to help your loved ones. Paradoxically, the more you care for yourself, the better you can help your loved ones. On this foundation, you are more likely to decrease enabling and to increase the likelihood of your loved one becoming sober. Let us now focus on the heart of helping: our *spiritual* dimension.

Chapter Nine

SPIRITUALITY: THE WAY TO RECOVERY

Spirituality is the foundation and sustaining source of recovery for ourselves and loved ones. Without rooting ourselves in the Reality who is both greater than and part of ourselves—rooting ourselves in our Holy Spirit—we wither and weaken. With God's presence, we are nurtured and strengthened. Alone, life becomes hell; with God, the kingdom comes regardless of what our loved ones do.

To be spiritual is not easy. It means going beyond our culture's cult of postmodern individualism and rationalism. Drawing on spiritual resources means that we transcend individualism to be with a God who is both infinitely more than and perpetually part of us. Our relationship with God includes and goes beyond our rational comprehension. It is grounded in love, evokes faith, and engenders hope.

To propose that our relationship with God is the core of better manageability and recovery is not only countercultural; it is also contrary to the mainstream of the social sciences. Until recently, there has been very little room for God in the houses of psychiatry, psychology, counseling, and social work. But contrary to what some contend, God and the spiritual life are *not* illusions or machinations of our minds.

A Higher Power, whom I call God, can help us be more successful in dealing with alcohol or other problems. When we depend only on ourselves or on rationality without God, we decrease our efficacy and increase our problems.

However we choose to construe the term *Higher Power*, prayer is essential to recovery. Whether our prayers are formal or informal, silent or verbal, private or shared—whether our intentions are those of thanksgiving, petition, praise, or penance—we must connect with God in order to gain true serenity. Relating to a Higher Power through prayer and meditation simply works better than relying solely on ourselves. Indeed, God is our saving grace.

A MOTHER'S PRAYER

Listen to Louise:

"When my daughter-in-law told me that she was planning to leave my son because of his drinking, I didn't know what to do. I didn't realize that he had gotten that bad. My son is a physician with a wonderful wife, two children, and a world of opportunities, but his life is falling apart. How could alcohol do that?

"After listening to my son, pleading with him, bribing him, screaming at him, withdrawing from him, I felt miserable, depressed, and powerless. Although I'm not especially religious, somehow I came to think about God. If I couldn't make a difference, maybe God could.

"I started to ask God to help me help my son. In time I actually learned to put our family in God's care. Somehow, surrendering myself and my son, daughter-in-law, and grandchildren to God gave me peace. It was strange: doing *less* helped me to do *more*.

"Putting all of us in God's care helped me to worry less and gave me the clarity and strength to accept reality as it is, not the way I wanted it to be. With God, I came to love and cope more compassionately and effectively."

TIME TO LET GO

Another reason spiritual life can be difficult is that we must let go of our ego control; that is, our well-intentioned attempts to manipulate. Like Louise, we usually let God into our lives—truly let him in—only after admitting that our solo efforts are making things worse. It is often at our lowest point that we finally look up. Like the alcoholic, we too usually have to hit bottom, when nothing seems to work and the misery is unbearable, in order to turn ourselves over to a Higher Power. Our challenge is to learn to turn to God *before* we experience such devastating pain and damage.

Surrendering to God does *not* mean that we abdicate responsibility and expect God to take care of everything. Rather, *we work with God*. We learn to live and act not as *me*, but as *we*—God-I-others. Then, regardless of your loved one's behavior, you can come to a new way of living, one that includes less fear, insecurity, sadness, and misery, and progressively more courage, confidence, joy, and serenity. Even in the middle of chaos you can experience a new order and freedom. Prayer is the primary way to achieve these promises.

PRAY TO BE PRAYERFUL

When you think, feel, and act alone, you weaken yourself. With God, you are significantly more effective in helping yourself and your loved one. Let us discuss more about this relationship between God and us in the context of alcoholic drinking.

Helen is discouraged:

"I've prayed my head off, until I was sick to my stomach. I go to church every day, and I pray and pray and pray that my husband will stop drinking and work on our marriage. But life just gets more and more tense, cold, and distant. I'm lonely; I just want relief.

"I pray that I'll get through the day with some semblance of sanity. I pray that I won't get angry and say things I later regret. I get so mad at myself for being mad. I pray that God will cure John. Pray? You better believe I pray. What more can I do?"

Like most spouses of alcoholics, Helen has had her dreams shattered. She had not planned on spending the remaining years of her life feeling frustrated, angry, and lonely. Unlike most others, she still goes to church daily and asks for God's help. For that, she is to be commended. And yet, there are still areas of Helen's life where there may be room for further growth.

AMPLIFYING OUR PRAYER

As we have seen, when someone we love drinks too much, the temptation is to invest too much of our time in, and spend too much energy on, the other person, pleading or arguing with him or her to stop drinking. With good intentions, we try to do the impossible to change the alcoholic. Sometimes out of futility, we withdraw and simply care for ourselves. In both cases, our love is genuine but misguided and one-sided. Rather than focusing solely on *you* or on *me*, a more effective way to love a drinker (or anyone) is to focus on *us*. Rather than just the drinker's welfare or my welfare, our love can be oriented to *our* welfare.

Like many people in her situation, Helen spends most of her prayer time pleading with God to change her husband. And yet, we have already seen that God is just as interested in *changing Helen* as in *changing her husband*. Life continually reminds us that we cannot need a person, even our spouse, to change in order to be happy.

By changing the focus of her prayer from *him* and *me* to *us*, things are more likely to improve for both of them. By changing herself, Helen helps her husband. The only person you can change is yourself, and the more you improve, the more your situation improves.

Although this dear woman does pray for herself, much of her prayer centers around purging her so-called negative feelings; in a sense, getting rid of parts of herself. Actually, she may be at odds with herself, which worsens her situation. She can learn to insert her wounded self in God's comforting and healing love. With God, this woman can embrace her pain. She can ask God to help her to accept, to listen to, and to learn from her troubling feelings. In love, she can begin to treat herself differently, and learn how her feelings can help her and her husband come to sobriety.

Helen prays probably more than most people. She prays before and after difficult times—and this is *good*. However, like most of us, Helen forgets to pray *during* the tough times. Our challenge is to pray not only before and after we are with our lovable drinker, but also and especially *when* we are with him or her. Along with preparing for and taking stock after troublesome situations, we can also connect with God when our loved one hurts us or pushes our buttons. In this way, Helen, and the rest of us, learns what it means to be prayerful.

For example, when your loved one refuses to admit to drinking too much, instead of arguing or trying to make him or her own up to the truth, pause and ask God to speak to your hearts—both yours and your loved one's. Before doing anything, insert yourself and your loved one in Love/God. Ask God to strengthen, protect, comfort, and guide you *when* you are with your functional alcoholic. Evoke and resonate with the Holy Spirit who dwells within both you and your loved one. Instead of your well-being depending on the drinker, depend on God. Instead of placing your serenity in precarious hands, cradle yourself in the palms of God's love.

So, rather than looking outside yourself, look within and connect with God's Spirit. Rather than reacting to your loved one's disrespect and lack of understanding, you can choose to "do" nothing except to simply "be" with God. Rather than needing your loved one to change and therefore to trying to manipulate him or her, you can accept in love your excessive drinker and detach from his or her maddening behavior.

GOD'S COMMUNITY OF LOVE

Bonding with God, or prayer, is paramount. And yet, it is also important to connect with healthy people who love us. Remember that God and people are dynamically interrelated. We should not try to be separate them. Although loving people are not always physically available, they, with God, are available *within* us. And so, when times are difficult, we can choose to imagine ourselves inside God's community of love—giving to and receiving from God, self, and others the power of love we need each day.

Dwelling in the community of love that perpetually abides within us does not solve everything or, for that matter, anything. However, dwelling in the power of love *does* strengthen us so that we do not "need" anything from the drinker, and yet we prefer, and remain open to, the possibility of receiving love, respect, honesty, reliability, accountability, and so on. With God and God's people, we can accept and cope with all circumstances with serenity, whether or not our preferences are met.

Although being in the community of love does not mean that everything is all right or that we do not hurt, life does get better, and we hurt less severely and less often. On a scale of 10, your pain falls from a 10, 9, or 8 to a 5, 4, or 3. With the infinite power of God's love, your pain is more manageable—and you are more able and willing to improve yourself and help your loved ones.

So we pray to be prayerful—to be in God's presence everywhere and always. After all, our nature is from and through God, and it is to be with and for God. Thus, when we are with God, we are really being true to ourselves. Indeed, this is easier said than done. But it *can* be done, and when it happens, everyone benefits—including the drinker.

In short, when you are prayerful when your loved one is drinking alcoholically, pushing your buttons, trying to manipulate you, frustrating or provoking you, alienating or saddening you, you are less likely to look to the drinker for your well-being, and more likely to place yourself in God's loving community.

Being in the presence of God's community of love, you are less likely to need your loved one to change and more likely to accept and love him or her, while never condoning alcoholic behavior. Grounded in love, you are empowered to set boundaries that minimize pain and maximize effective coping. In God, you can give what you want to receive. Ideally, you can manifest and offer love to the drinker.

Our challenge is to live in, with, and through love for and from God, self, and others in both the good and bad, high and low, happy and sad, light and dark, laughing and tearful, in life and in death. Love is for all seasons.

Love exists for imperfect people—and, admittedly, some of us are more imperfect than others! If we were perfect, we would not need love; we would be forever in love, in heaven. Indeed, we get glimpses of heaven, but we are on earth where people we love simply drink too much.

Chapter Ten

WHERE IS GOD?

"It kills me to watch my wife slowly disappear. Although she always drank, she seemed to have it under control. She always met her responsibilities for being a mother. Sure, sometimes she got pretty high, but I got a kick out of it. In fact, I'd join her because she was more fun with alcohol. But as we got older, she drank more, and I drank less. When the kids reached their late teens, she put her drinking in overdrive and increased her speed.

"Look, I pray a lot, more than most men I know. I never stopped saying the Divine Office [the Liturgy of the Hours] from my monastic days. I pray, but I don't know where God is. He's not answering my prayers. Why? I've lived a good life. I know I'm not being punished for leaving the monastery. After all, I was a good monk and had not yet professed permanent vows.

"So, what's going on? Where is God? Why doesn't he make my wife stop drinking? Why doesn't he make her the woman I thought I married? Why does he allow this to go on? I know men who have not lived as good a life as I and some who have been unfaithful, and they have sober, loving wives. What's the use of praying? Those men seldom pray, and they have a better life.

"Sure, my wife still loves me, but how! Have you ever made love with someone who has been drinking too much? It wasn't so bad when we were both drinking, but now everything's out of sync. She's so volatile: She can laugh and suddenly cry and then withdraw. I never know how she will react.

"God, where are you? I can identify with Christ's words on his cross—'My God, My God, why have you forsaken me!'"

Some of us feel God is more absent than present. We feel forsaken, and, especially when we have prayed, we feel abandoned. Was Freud right? Is God an illusion? Is God opium for people who cannot reason? What can we do when we pray and nothing happens? What can we do when we find ourselves lost in the middle of the desert looking for the promised land?

A CRY IN THE DESERT

The first thing we can do may be the most difficult; namely, to do *nothing*, to let ourselves just *be* in the desert. Like Job, we can express our frustration, anger, and fear to God. At other times, we can sit, listen, and wait. Rather than following a false god like alcohol, other drugs, sex, or work, we can be *steadfast*, *patient*, and *still*. It may be difficult to accept that *patience* is the best and *fastest* way to God. In these days of immediate gratification, patience is a difficult and lost art. In patience, we are challenged to be and act according to God's time, not ours.

When nothing seems to make sense and God seems to have disappeared, we need hope more than ever. In fact, hope makes little sense without potential or actual despair, or at least without radical doubt. During these dark times, it is important to remain open to life's possibilities. Rather than allowing our expectations and needs to constrict us, we remain available to God's way. We must trust that, not infrequently, the greatest joys come out of suffering, strength out of weakness, faith out of doubt. Hope often blossoms in the desert of despair.

Along with *patience* and *hope*, the desert of doubt calls for *faith* and *trust*. Our challenge is to accept that which we cannot rationally understand or explain—why God *seems* to have abandoned us. Feeling forsaken, how do we not give up? We must remember that although we are powerless, we are not helpless. We can do some things in response to our nothingness. *We can act in order to improve how we feel.*

We can reach out to people who have made it out of their own dark pit of despair. We can seek those who really know and who can enter into our suffering. We can trust and hold on to the people who have made it through the desert of abandonment. They offer help that comes from their experiences, not simply theories. Their experience, strength, and hope form a bond with us and lead us to a promised land of meaning, consolation, and purpose.

Such people are always important, especially when we are in the throes of desolation. They have managed and grown through their suffering to become bearers and sharers of God. They are sources of guidance, support, compassion, and consolation. They offer freedom, serenity, and love. Theoretically, these loving warriors can be found anywhere. More likely, they dwell in the rooms of 12-step meetings and other holy places.

Like the father of the prodigal son (Luke 15:11–32), we are called to be hopeful and patient. We wait for our loved ones to emerge out of the decadence of drinking, and we see and run to meet them on the horizon of sobriety, so that we may embrace them in love. In time, this reconciliation will happen, often in this life, but sometimes only in the next. Your desire for God actually exists in doubt, questioning, disillusionment, frustration, powerlessness. Your loneliness implies and seeks love. Emptiness affirms and desires fulfillment. And nothing but God will satisfy your desire for God.

As 12-steppers would say, sometimes we "have to fake it in order to make it." Out of respect for and trust of sober and healthy people, we practice what works. And in time, we become what we do. The truth is that when we practice patience, hope, trust, and love, they become good habits. Being integral parts of us, they motivate us to be patient with ourselves and loved ones, to hope and trust that with God almost anything is possible, and to live in love no matter what happens. Then we find ourselves leaving the desert and entering the promised land.

TURNING YOUR BACK ON GOD

When you watch your loved one displace God and yourself with alcohol, and when you ask God to help and seemingly get no answers, you may be tempted to turn your back on God. It is understandable and not an uncommon reaction to abandon God and even your loved ones, and to simply take care of yourself.

False assumptions often play a part in our divorce from God. For instance, we may assume that if we live a good and God-centered life, life will be good to us, God will automatically solve our problems, and God will make our loved one sober. Or that if we pray in the "right" way, our needs will be satisfied and nothing bad will happen to us. Or if we are holy, our loved one will see and follow the light and become sober. These and similar assumptions set us up for disappointment and discouragement.

Many people love the Serenity Prayer. You may have seen it with slightly different words, but here is one of the most widely used versions:

> God grant me
> the serenity to accept the things I cannot change,
> courage to change the things I can,
> and wisdom to know the difference.

This is the main prayer of Alcoholics Anonymous and other 12-step programs because it *truly* makes sense. Here's why:

God grant me

- the serenity to accept the things I cannot change
  (*my alcoholic loved one, other problematic loved ones, even my own alcoholic drinking*),
- courage to change the things I can (*myself*),
- and wisdom to know the difference (*between who and what I can and cannot change*).

In short, *prayer empowers us to accept and to do God's will.* Still, alcoholism as well as any unhealthy or bad behaviors endangers our health and serenity. So what could God's will be for us, for how we respond, in the travails of any abusive behavior?

- Maybe our loved one's behavior humbles us to grow and be more dependent on God.

- Maybe God is asking the more fortunate and stronger ones to take care of the less fortunate and weaker ones.
- Maybe suffering calls for compassionate care to improve our lives of love.
- Maybe our call is to form a community that includes all people, sober or not.
- Maybe we would be diminished without them.
- Maybe we are all different and necessary threads of the same tapestry.
- Maybe our problems can pressure us to improve our own lives and thus to be better persons.
- Maybe the absurd affirms that there *is* another life where we will live together in love.

Chapter Eleven

HOW DO YOU LOVE?

What does it mean to love a functional alcoholic? For certain, it means pain: disappointment, frustration, loneliness, depression, fear, and anxiety.

How do you love in the middle of hell? Why care? What is love? What part does our Higher Power of Love/God play? Your responses to these and similar questions will significantly influence if you survive in hell on earth, or thrive more in heaven on earth.

Probably no other topic gets more attention than love. Indeed, much of music, theater, and literature involves love. Numerous philosophical, theological, spiritual, psychological, sociological, and literary analyses have differentiated the nature, dynamics, and kinds of love. Religion and spirituality are about love. Life is essentially about love.

How you construe love will highly influence the way you treat yourself and others. For instance, when a married couple has very different views of what it means to love and be loved, serious problems will occur. And when one of the spouses is a drinker, love is severely tested. Let us look at love in regards to alcoholism or, if you want, any problematic situation.

EMPATHIC LOVE

For many people, love involves doing what is best for others, trying to make them happy. Self-sacrifice, sufferance, self-minimization, and deference to others are symptomatic of empathic love.

When we err on the empathic end of the love continuum, we are apt to try to care through pleasing, overt enabling, and satisfying the drinker's needs at our own expense. We try to accept, understand, and love unconditionally, falsely assuming that our "perfect" love will change the other. To that end, we are vulnerable to taking responsibility for others as well as taking their blame and guilt. We feel that if only we loved better, things would change for the better. Indeed, we actually facilitate and foster the very thing we want changed.

We silently chant to ourselves: "Perfect love solves all problems. If I understand, affirm, and nurture my drinker, he or she will surely change for the better. What more can I do? There must be an answer. And if perchance things do not improve, then I will surely get a high place in heaven."

Such well-intentioned and caring persons unknowingly assume that they have more power than they really have. Even the greatest spiritual leaders could not, nor would they try to, "make" people be better or to heal them without their cooperation. Their power was appeal, not force; co-creation, not manipulation.

NARCISSISTIC LOVE

At the other end of this love continuum is love that maximizes one's *own* welfare and minimizes the other's. With such "self-love," we are prone to care for ourselves at the exclusion and expense of others. We look out for *numero uno.* "Your problems are not mine," we declare. Whatever our relationship—husband and wife, parent and child, friend and friend, sibling and sibling—it is in trouble.

When we err on the narcissistic side of love, we are likely to blame and be overtly angry at the drinker. Instead of using methods of seduction, we try to force and threaten our functional alcoholic to get clean and sober. Unlike the empathic lover, we blame the other for our misery and abdicate our own part in it. Our laments include: "It's *his* fault I'm so unhappy"…"If only *she* would change, then I'd feel better"…"*You're* to blame for my misery"… "Why can't *you* be like me?" Clearly, as long as we fail to admit responsibility and persist in focusing on the faults and deficits of the other, improvement is unlikely.

DOUBLE-STANDARD LOVE

Many of us harbor double standards for love: those we hold for others and those we hold over our own heads. All too often, we love ourselves less adequately than we love others. Consequently, we judge ourselves more harshly than others whom we judge more kindly and fairly. We tend to be more accepting, understanding, and forgiving of others than we are to ourselves. This is especially true if you are a pleaser or perfectionist.

We have seen that unless you love yourself and seek love from God and God's people, you are apt to look to a person who may be unable to love consistently and wholeheartedly. Actually, you are not only being terribly unfair to yourself but also to the problem person, for you *make* him or her the source of your happiness. Keep in mind that the alcoholic or any disturbed person has more than enough problems without your own. Once again, trying to acquire bread at a hardware store only makes matters worse for both you and the others.

When you insert yourself in the community of love dwelling within you, you are better able to love, help, and improve yourself. Then, instead of reacting with overly emphatic, narcissistic, or passive-aggressive care, you can respond with healthy and often tough love.

HEALTHY KINDS OF LOVE

Healthy love means love that can choose to think of, and choose to do, what is best for *us*—not just you or just me. Healthy love fosters the welfare of community. In love, we strive to be and do well. We promote what brings people together, and avoid what tears people apart. We desire to bring unity to separateness, peace to war, healing to disease, warmth to coldness, compassion to suffering, trust to distrust, and intimacy to isolation.

In love, we realize that we are differently colored, sized, aged, gendered, and gifted; we are stronger and weaker threads of the same evolving tapestry. God who dwells within us desires that we weave and enhance the tapestry of humankind so that it manifests goodness and beauty. All the threads, including the frayed and ugly, have a place in this tapestry. Without them, our human tapestry would not be as strong and rich. We would be diminished. In the tapestry of humankind, there is no *we vs. them* dichotomy; there is only *us*. So, where and how are the threads of alcoholics and other disruptive persons woven in this human tapestry?

To love a drinker (or any addict) is an enormous and unending challenge. It is difficult enough to love when someone loves you, but when that someone loves another (alcohol) more than you, love is daunting. It takes a very special love—one that is tough, suffering, detached, and unconditional.

TOUGH LOVE

In our efforts to perfect love, we will experience our limits and imperfections, for we are always becoming or in the process of perfecting ourselves. We are forever growing in love, happiness, peace, faith, and other virtues, and therefore will at times be lonely, unhappy, restless, doubtful, or less than perfectly virtuous. In short, we will hurt: We will be incomplete, anxious, lost, less then serene until we rest perpetually in Divine Love. St. Augustine said it truly is his *Confessions*: "We will always be restless until we rest in Thee, O God."

Living perpetually and perfectly in love is heaven, where we will finally abide in the serenity of Divine Love. On earth, we desire this promised place where we are always one with God, but we only get glimpses of, and fleeting feelings for, this sacred place. Our restless and restive feelings affirm that we are always on our way to "getting it," and yet they motivate us to seek being one with Love.

However, on earth our love can be wounded, our oneness broken. We struggle to be "one with" but often end up distant or apart. We hide and hold rather than disclose and share. When you love *any* human being (and especially a drinker), you *will* get hurt. In love, you more or less expose and offer your most precious and vulnerable part of yourself. Indeed, the healthier and more perfected your love is, the less you will be hurt. *But no love on earth is perfect.*

There are many ways to avoid or minimize being hurt. We can achieve temporary respite from hurt by repressing our feelings or, like the drinker, using alcohol or drugs. We can run from hurtful situations via work, reading, sex, television, or the Internet. Though sometimes necessary, fixating on such behavior impedes and can seriously violate love and therefore life. Thus, we have to learn to practice so-called tough love that comes from bonding with the Source of Love. However, tough love is "tough" to do.

Part of the challenge of tough love is accepting and even fostering an ability and willingness to suffer for another person's sake. To be criticized unjustly, to be mocked and shamed, to be the target of cruelty, to be ignored, are all very painful. Still, when you empower and console yourself with the Higher Power of God's love, you can protect and perfect yourself.

Tough love means letting the drinker deal with the consequences of his (or her) behavior, letting him be in pain, setting boundaries, and giving choices. Out of love, we can be clear about what we will and will *not* tolerate. Although we love the drinker no matter what, we do not accept unacceptable behavior. Tough love means taking a stand—and sticking to it.

It takes tough love not to collude with family and friends who deny your spouse's alcoholic drinking. Standing in God's love enables you to stand firm in love when your spouse begs you to cover for him when he misses work, seduces you to act against your morals, or simply wants you to enable his drinking. We need self-love rooted in God in order to keep behavioral standards, to consistently give consequences for unacceptable behavior, and to reward good behavior.

Without standing in the strength of God's love, tough love becomes an exhausting exercise in will power. However, we can stand in the power and protection of God's love for others and us.

DETACHED LOVE

Detached love may sound like an oxymoron, for love means attachment. But in reality, when you love a problem person, both attachment and detachment are needed.

Detachment can involve a number of postures and activities. Fundamentally, detachment means that we disengage from our enmeshed relationship so that we no longer depend on dependent people (functional alcoholics). Instead of being inordinately attached to any human, place, thing, or activity, we attach to Love/God. Such attachment enables us to accept and detach from harmful behavior.

Think of when someone upsets you. Do you react with anger, appeasement, or withdrawal? Such common reactions are ineffective, and usually only make matters worse. Rather than "reacting," it is better and more effective first to pause and bond with the love that dwells within you—with love for and from God, self, and others. Part of this power is that nobody, except you, can tamper with it. When you draw on the power of this love, you can decide how to care in ways that detach from painful behavior.

For instance, you need not take the alcoholic behavior too personally. Even though it may be directed at you, you can remind yourself that if you died, the drinker would continue to behave the same way. He would soon find new targets to replace you. To expect a drinker to behave differently is unrealistic. Again, it is going to the hardware store for bread. When you detach from your loved one's behavior, you will hurt less, be stronger, enable less, and feel better.

Consider when a problem person tries to provoke an argument by accusing, demeaning, or insulting you. Naturally, your defenses go up, and you may retaliate and hurt back (thus evening the score: zero to zero). Or you absorb the attack and plead guilty to false charges. In the aggressive attack and the passive absorbing modes, you accomplish little of positive value. Actually, you risk diminishing yourself.

In such situations, healthy detachment means that you first attach to your Higher Power of Love/God. On and in this power base, you can refuse to get sucked into futile behavior that only increases your pain. You can remind yourself of the analogy of the pooping pigeons—namely, that is what problem people do. Protecting yourself within the boundaries of self-love in God, you can consider the source of your abuse and expect nothing more or less. You can detach yourself by not taking the abuse too personally, even though it is *meant* to be personal. Your secret is that your worth comes from within you, and *not* from a person who is unwilling or unable to treat you with respect.

Detachment can be external, internal, or both. Sometimes it is wise to detach physically. When under fire or stressed, you might go to your room or the bathroom, get out and take a walk, or escape to a friend's house. Such physical detachment can give you the time and space to settle within your spiritual center as well as to recollect your thoughts and coping skills.

Sometimes physical separation is a necessary form of tough love. *Allowing* yourself to be abused only harms you and enables the drinker. In this case, no one is helped. You might need to leave your spouse in order to survive. Or, you might have to send your teenager to a residential program for drug abusers. It is common to feel guilty for obtaining relief by no longer living with a disruptive person. Yet, although you may feel sad, guilt is inappropriate. Be instead, *grateful*. Such physical separation can be a wonderful opportunity not only for the drug abuser, but for you, too. When away from your loved one, you can take the opportunity to recover your own health, to normalize your life.

Even more important than physical detachment is psychological and spiritual detachment, which, as we have seen, is based on internal attachment. For example, you can learn to "detach" from your worry or obsessive thoughts, and "attach" to some other thoughts. You can learn to meditate with a mantra—a word or phrase that helps you get your mind off itself and on to something settling and liberating. For many, saying and savoring the Serenity Prayer brings (not surprisingly!) serenity.

Listen to this man's story of detachment:

"Soon after the New Year announced itself, I retired to bed. However, my wife was upset and worried about our teenaged daughter, who had a curfew. My wife criticized me for not caring. My view was that I did care, but differently. For me, to worry and pace only exhausted me and didn't do any good. I thought if I got some sleep, I would be in better shape to help our daughter when she eventually showed up.

"To be sure, sleep was not easy. What helped was that I learned to repeat a mantra ('Let go and let God') that helped me detach from my worry and attach to Divine Providence, which enabled me to sleep. Actually, I have a 'thirteen-second rule.' If I obsess for more than thirteen seconds, I defocus from my worry and refocus on a mantra. Look, if worry did any good, I'd worry my head off. But it doesn't, and moreover it causes more difficulty.

"Anyhow, our daughter finally got home at 7:30 a.m. My wife, who never slept, was furiously hysterical, shouting at, demeaning, and threatening our daughter. I think I was in better shape to avoid arguing and focus clearly and firmly on the main issue—her extreme behavior. I simply think that getting rest allowed me to handle the situation better."

You may think that this example is unrealistic or impossible to follow—but not really. Like this man, you can learn to detach and thereby take better care of both yourself and your loved ones.

Detachment with love means that you can sit in the audience with God and watch the drama of drinking. Although your loved one may beckon you to get on the stage and be part of the play, you can *refuse* to play the role of the enabler, and *detach with love*. Without your role, the drama must change. Without applauding or booing, you let the new play unfold. Such love is tough, for it takes courage and compassion.

Chapter Twelve

THE COURAGEOUS WAY OF COMPASSION

Someone once said that "courage is fear that has said its prayers." If we were not vulnerable, if we could not be hurt, and if we had perfect love, we would not need courage.

Allowing yourself to be vulnerable in love, giving without expectation of return, and caring for the drinker takes courage.

Pointing out a drinker's alcoholic thinking, setting boundaries for acceptable and unacceptable behavior, voicing feelings of hurt and fear, refusing to shrink in the middle of aggressive reasoning, and risking criticism and rejection takes courage.

Interacting with your loved one without aggression or submission and with assertive kindness and justice takes courage.

We have seen that accepting what we cannot change is essential for serenity. Controlling and changing ourselves (which is all that we *can* change) calls for courage. We need courage to modify our beliefs and attitudes, our style of caring for ourselves and others, our coping strategies, our relationships with people and with God, and perhaps even our reason for being. Courage is needed because these kinds of changes engender uncertainty, anxiety, and fear. To be in a state of "not-yetness," to step into the unknown, and to change are courageous decisions and acts.

GOD: OUR SOURCE OF COURAGE

Courage cannot exist without God's grace.

With God, we find ourselves being the person we never were, and doing things we never tried or that frightened us. When we rely solely on ourselves, we weaken ourselves, and yet when we own up to our powerlessness, we are motivated to seek a Higher Power. When God dwells in our hearts, we discover the courage to change who and what we can.

Listen to this courageous woman:

"I was always a silent sufferer. I sucked it in and swallowed myself. I followed my mother's dictum that since I chose my bed of nails, I must lie in it. 'Nobody put a gun to your head and forced you to marry that man,' I can hear her say.

"I got used to being alone, playing third fiddle to alcohol. I got used to satisfying my husband's needs, to running the house, to taking care of the kids, to making excuses for him, to agreeing with him, to avoiding conflict. And yet, I felt that I was losing my dignity and that life should be better.

"After I had endured years of minimal living, one of my friends asked me to go on a retreat. Of course, I said I was too busy and my husband wouldn't like it, but she pursued and persuaded me and her care touched me. Ironically or providentially, the subject of the retreat was the 'courage to change.'

"Away from my restricted and fearful life and in the freedom and security of solitude and fellowship, I saw some light in my darkness; I heard the whisper of a permanent reprieve from my life sentence. A better life felt possible. For the first time, I felt the love of God embrace me and somehow encourage me to change. When I got home, I found myself in courage, or encouraged.

"In the presence of God, I began to behave differently with my husband. I no longer agreed with him when I really disagreed. I didn't argue; I simply stated my position. I learned to say a new word: *No*. I stopped shrinking. Somehow my fear of my husband dissipated, and I felt taller and stronger. I learned that feeling weaker and smaller was a cue for me to pray. In a sense, I used my weakness to gain strength. So when my husband would push my old buttons, I would call on God.

"My husband didn't know what to do with my new behavior. Initially, he actually drank more and withdrew into blatant alcoholism. With God's help, I let him take the consequences of his drinking. And I learned to have a fuller life regardless of my husband. Sure, I would rather have him with me, but it wasn't necessary.

"Incredibly, I think he became afraid of me. He was and still is confused. Unfortunately, I think he's trying to find his courage in a bottle instead of in God and her people. After much praying and sharing, I came to believe that God wanted me to divorce him. So I did and finally became more of the woman God intended me to be."

Indeed, God is *the* source of courage. Like this woman, *you* can experience God helping you make right decisions and, if necessary, divorce physically and psychologically. With God and people, you can focus on yourself and learn to cope with, and grow stronger through, the fears and anxieties of change.

Courage is God helping you to be and to live in ways that you never thought were possible. With God, what you thought was impossible becomes possible. Paradoxically, when you admit to and share your fears, limits, and anxieties, you will find courage, freedom, and serenity instead.

THE COMPASSIONATE HEART

Being compassionate with someone who hurts you is a supreme test and manifestation of love. When we are hurt, we tend to react with "fight or flight" or even simply freeze. Sometimes aggression or withdrawal is needed, but ideally it is better to stand strong, remembering God's love.

Compassion does not mean to pity or patronize the other. As compassionate people, we begin on the same plane as our loved ones, not higher or lower. Standing with and for our brothers and sisters, we enter their worlds to see how reality looks from their perspective. Neither condemning nor condoning, we get a feel for how they experience life. Without judgment, we listen and try to understand.

Our empathic stance enables us to help people bear the weight of their existence. Our goal is not to purge them of their pain. Nevertheless, being with them in their pain can lighten their burden. Being alone in pain is hell, but being with someone else in pain is more like purgatory—a transition to a better place. When you let yourself be touched with compassion, it kindles inside you a hopeful vision. When you realize that you are no longer alone, you can discover the courage to change.

WARRIORS IN THE DARKNESS

Relating to and following the supreme compassion of God, we find the courage to enter the underworld of troubled people. With God protecting and sustaining us, we are able to embrace them in their darkness.

Remember that our loved ones often hide their "shameful self" behind a protective wall of alcohol, hiding not only from us but from themselves as well. In the throes of shame, they want to disappear, and alcohol numbs the pain of their shame. Although our loved ones who are full of shame may never clasp our helping hands, we can continue to see them with compassionate eyes.

As compassionate people, we have faced and fought many battles. We have been wounded, we have cared for ourselves, and we have become strong. Pain, evil, danger, injustice, and shame are not strangers to us. Paradoxically, it is this fact that allows us to help those who hurt us and to manage them with strength and integrity.

But compassion *is* difficult. We must train to be "loving warriors." We must develop and practice love that is unconditional and empathic. *But love is not enough.* We must also be warriors— to have the courage to face and deal with the drinker's dark side. Rather than denying or running away from the ugly and painful parts of drinking, we face the embarrassing behavior and offer our love to the shameful self. We offer compassionate love instead of alcohol.

To be compassionate, we must face our own darkness. It takes courage and compassion to shed the light of healing truth on our own neediness, fears, narcissism, greed, ignorance, anger, and shame. This loving purgation is necessary because we cannot see in others what we avoid in ourselves. In fact, we are likely to project on to the drinker what we cannot accept in ourselves. Instead of light, we cast darkness on darkness. When we respond lovingly to our own wounds, when we are compassionate with ourselves, we can become "wounded healers," to use Henri Nouwen's term.

To gain the courage and strength of a loving warrior, as well as the humble and healing touch of a wounded healer, we must immerse ourselves in God's community of love. Even though the drinker may be mean, we know that he or she is an integral member of the same "kind" as us—of humankind.

Even though our drinking brethren may weaken our common body, they are still our brothers and sisters. Out of compassion, their relative weakness challenges us to be loving warriors. We strive to offer our embrace to our prodigal spouse, child, parent, brother, sister, or friend.

In compassion, we recognize and appreciate that all of us, drinkers or not, are pilgrims on a journey that includes many deserts and promised lands. When we feel lost in that desert, trapped in the prison of abuse, this community of love gives us strength to lift ourselves out of the dark pit to see the light of possibilities. Our burdens grow lighter. Someone knows how we feel. *Being known in love is redemptive.*

Compassionate love is one way that God shows you divine care and helps you carry the burdens of being forsaken. God will probably not take away your struggles, or magically and instantly remove all your pain (albeit God *might!*). Instead God offers you help to cope, gives you courage, encourages your choices, and laughs and cries with you. God struggles with you to heal in a broken world, and often without your knowing, God carries you along the way.

God is all-compassionate. God suffers with you, lightens your burdens, heals your wounds, and comforts and consoles you. In, with, and through God and God's people, you can come to new life.

Chapter Thirteen

"How Can I Forgive?"

"I don't know if I'll ever forgive him, or if I even want to. Yet I know, at least I'm told, it's better to forgive, but it's *not* easy. I don't know—to forgive or not to forgive; both are tough.

"It was so hard to understand when our pastor announced that he was taking an extended leave to go to rehab for his alcohol problem. I thought of all the times he had been to my home, of how often I shared my brokenness with this man. He was not just my pastor; he was also a friend of the family. I admired and trusted this man, and now I feel he's let me down, almost betrayed me. I feel like a fool. He is not the man I thought I knew.

"You're sure right, I'm angry. Wouldn't you be? This man was preaching the good news and challenging us to follow the way of Christ. Did he practice what he preached? What a hypocrite!

"In a way, I feel I am to blame for his drinking. When I asked him what he wanted for a gift, he casually said alcohol. I think of how stupid I was in serving him alcohol, or in making excuses for him when he got a bit tipsy. I'm not sure if I'm angrier with him or with me especially when I think of how he lied to me. I should have known better. Still, I feel he used me. And yet, I doubt myself. How do I move past this?"

This woman's feelings are natural and understandable. She feels that her pastor deceived and used her. She is disillusioned, resentful, and guilty. She senses that her feelings can devour her and rob her of her integrity and serenity. She also feels that she can no longer trust and feel at home in her church. And when *your* loved one is even closer than a friend or minister, *you* hurt even more.

Forgiveness is another difficult but important virtue to practice. Without forgiveness, we tread water with a millstone around our neck. At worst, resentment can consume us like a terminal cancer. It is hard enough to forgive your loved ones when they have stopped drinking and become sober, but to forgive someone who *still* currently abuses you is indeed a sublime and daunting test of love. Without connecting with our Higher Power, such forgiveness becomes virtually impossible.

We have seen or heard about people who have forgiven those who gravely hurt them—and those who have not. Think of the mother who forgives her child's abuser, the husband who forgives the drunken driver who disfigured his wife, or the woman who forgives her abusive ex-husband. We also think of spiritual icons like Jesus Christ, who suggested and showed how to forgive endlessly. So what does it mean to forgive someone whose drinking hurts us?

Although forgiveness is one of the most important experiences in achieving serenity, it is often misunderstood. Let us first reflect on what forgiveness is not.

WHAT FORGIVENESS DOES *NOT* MEAN

To forgive does not mean to forget. Actually, we should remember and learn how to deal with negative behavior so that if and probably when it reappears, we are ready to act effectively. To forget would be foolish.

To remember does not mean to harbor resentment. On the contrary, forgiveness frees us from bearing grudges and retaliating. Actually, *trying* to forget reinforces painful memories and exacerbates pain. And yet, when we truly forgive, current behavior and past memories bother us less. Forgiveness is as much for our own peace of mind as it is for the abuser. As its etymology suggests, forgiveness relieves us of the burdens of resentment, vindictiveness, or of needing justice.

To forgive does not imply condoning, rationalizing, excusing, or enabling immoral or destructive behavior. Instead of denying and repressing, you can face and deal with painful behavior and feelings. The challenge is to reject bad acts and to accept in love yourself and your loved one. Indeed, we must be sufficiently strong and secure in order *not* to need justice.

To forgive does not mean whitewashing the dark side of our own *lives*. It is not wiping the slate clean or making everything all right. Forgiveness is not a cure-all, but it does indeed heal. Forgiveness increases the likelihood that your loved ones will begin to admit to wrongdoings and make amends. Even more so, forgiveness enables *you* to be free from the shackles of needing the other to change and be sorry, and frees you for a better life.

WHAT FORGIVENESS *DOES* MEAN

Forgiveness can simply mean to accept ourselves and others in love. When we forgive our loved ones, we *give for* them. Our intent is not to make ourselves feel good (although this is usually a natural consequence), to manipulate them, or even "to get a high place in heaven." Our intent is to give to and for their and our welfare, which is the heart of reconciliation.

Think about it: *To be loved when you are at your best is great, but to be loved when you are at your worst is greater*. When we abstain from interrogating, criticizing, or patronizing, and compassionately embrace our loved ones, they (and we!) are more likely to feel accepted, consoled, reconciled, renewed, and healed.

Forgiveness increases the likelihood of consolation and reconciliation. When forgiven, we feel consoled (*com-* + *solari* = "comforted") rather than desolated (*de-* + *solus* = "alone"). Forgiveness restores our integrity (*integer* = wholeness) and dignity (*dignus* = worth), and in a sense we are reborn.

When we forgive our prodigal loved ones, we do not tell them to clean and shape themselves up, but like the biblical parent of the prodigal child, we can welcome them home as dirty and disordered. And if they do not return home, we continue to live the way God asks of us.

Forgiveness is also *fore*-giving: our healing love is ready to be given even *before* it is asked for—although, of course, it is probably easier and better for our loved ones if they do ask for forgiveness and try to make amends. But in some ways, it is even more important to forgive if it is not requested or is refused. Unrequited forgiveness affirms the dignity of your loved ones and invites them to be their better (sober) selves.

Remember that forgiving yourself is just as important as forgiving your abusers. Many of us forgive others better and more than we forgive ourselves. If you value others more than yourself, you may forget or not know how to forgive yourself.

"Why should I forgive myself?" you might ask. "After all, isn't the drinker the real culprit?"

While this may be true, we also have plenty to forgive in ourselves: our attempts (both overtly and covertly) to change and manipulate others, our failure to care for ourselves, our displacing God with our loved one. Unless we forgive ourselves, we will always be at odds with ourselves, even if our loved one becomes sober. We must make amends to ourselves primarily by caring for ourselves and living a better life.

GOD: THE ULTIMATE FORGIVER

All forgiveness—whether it is forgiving ourselves or forgiving another person—draws from God's forgiveness. The unconditional love of God is just, merciful, kind, and comforting. Indeed, God's love is made for imperfect people. We can depend on God to love us always and no matter what.

When we feel lower than we thought we could go, we can look up to a Divine Love who is there for us. When we are furious with God or when God feels absent, God is there for us. We must endure in the belief that anger, powerlessness, and absence can lead to the serenity, power, and presence that/who heals. "My God, why have you abandoned me?" When you cry out these words, know that you are on the verge of being embraced in love.

God loves our broken selves—accepts and embraces in his love our shame and woundedness. The help, hope, and healing of God's forgiveness are our saving grace and perhaps God's greatest gift to us. Regardless of whether your loved one stops drinking, God's forgiveness can comfort us and give us hope for a better day.

Chapter Fourteen

THE STRENGTH OF HUMILITY AND GRATITUDE

In addition to forgiveness, two other virtues are critical to our own recovery and that of alcoholics. The first virtue, humility, affirms our dependency on a Higher Power. Humility removes barriers that impede us from helping ourselves and our loved ones in their battle with alcohol. The second virtue, gratitude, fosters a conscious contact with God, engenders a healthy perspective, and enables us to receive the help that God wants to give us.

THE GIFT OF HUMILITY

Humility, like forgiveness, prevents us from taking ourselves too seriously, while freeing us to learn effective ways to improve ourselves and our loved ones. Most importantly, humility fosters a healthy relationship with God—the radical source of empowerment.

"Why be humble?" you might ask. You may feel sick and tired of being humble in putting up with your loved one's nonsense. Or, you might enjoy the rush of setting aside so-called humility in order to attack the enemy, to pay back a little of the pain you have received. Humility might naturally seem to be a bad idea. Let's take a closer look at what we mean by humility.

Sometimes the words *humility* and *humiliation* get confused because they share the same etymology: *humus* = "earth." Humiliation means to have our faces rubbed in the dirt. Humility places us in our appropriate place on earth—radically dependent on God.

Humility is not the same as humiliation. We need not flagellate, degrade, demean, or lessen ourselves. Many of us have a biased "committee" that resides within our conscience. It never accepts, listens, or comforts, but rather it rejects, criticizes, and humiliates. But we are never to debase our dignity and integrity, intentionally expose ourselves to insult, or allow ourselves to be violated. Not only do such acts of humiliation impede effective helping, they empower the drinker and foster impotence in ourselves.

Just as God does not want us to humiliate ourselves, neither does God want us to humiliate others, or make them less than they really are. That would be a violation of God's creation. Sometimes, it may be tempting to humiliate our loved ones, especially when they are being irritating or obnoxious. Remember: drinkers usually harbor considerable toxic shame and are consequently quite vulnerable to being humiliated. Besides fueling the fire of addiction, such behavior is cruel. Humiliation only harms and never helps.

When we are humble, we are less likely to assume that we have more power than we really do. We are less likely to try to fix the ones we love, or to manipulate them into sobriety. Humility enables us to accept, surrender to, and center our lives in a Greater Power that is infinitely greater than and yet part of ourselves. In pride, we give ourselves too much power and credit. In humility, we bow to and draw on a Greater Power. Being humble or down to earth enables us to look up and out to the greater power of God's love.

When we stop assuming that we have more power than we actually have, it becomes easier to listen to God's Spirit within us. We remove ourselves from the center and place God back in the center of our lives. Unlike humiliation, humility empowers us.

Humility means that we rely on God, not simply on ourselves. We ask God for help and remain open to God's guidance that pride blocks out. We humbly ask God to remove our shortcomings, especially those that impede being humble.

When we are humble we recognize that *we are all children of God*. We realize that we come from and are sustained by the same Source. We can bow to one another, even to the alcoholic, because we know we are all interrelated members of God's humankind.

Accepting our limits is a springboard to the Unlimited. And so our powerlessness over our loved one's drinking can be an opportunity to practice humility and consequently to improve our lives. Faced with the reality of our earthly limitations, we seek the unlimited God who promises a better life. In drawing on the Higher Power of Love, we reverently recognize that humility is a sign and source of strength.

THE GIFT OF GRATITUDE

"Grateful? *Grateful*? What do *I* have to be grateful for? I've slaved all my life, raising the children, taking care of the house, caring for our parents, and working part-time outside the home. Meanwhile, my alcohol-driven husband is always on center stage getting the applause, while I remain backstage making sure the show goes on. What do I have to be grateful for—frustration, fatigue, loneliness, disillusionment?"

It's one thing to be grateful for something that pleases us or that alleviates discomfort. But when life is at its worst, it seems cruel and sadistic to say that we need to practice gratitude. And yet this is often the very thing that will help us the most to feel better in the middle of turmoil. The truth is that there are always gifts for which we can be thankful. When we practice the attitude of gratitude, we are pressured to look for and appreciate those gifts—starting with the moment of conception to the present moment.

The Latin word for *gratitude* is connected to the word for *grace*—or, God's favor. In a sense, an attitude of gratitude links us to God; as we have seen, this is the core of equanimity and effective coping. When we practice gratitude, we remember the good that puts the negative in perspective, as well as puts more balance and peace in our lives. Gratitude invites us to slow down, to pause, and to recognize the plentitude of God's gifts—and, more importantly, to let them touch us. Gratitude brings enjoyment and peace, however fleeting. When we are in the pit of travail, gratitude offers us some reprise, comfort, and solace.

Try to make gratitude a daily habit. It could be something as simple as thinking of five things for which you can be thankful every night before retiring: friends and loved ones, food and shelter, work and play, a child and a puppy, the sun, moon, and stars....We realize that things could not only be much worse, but that, overall, life is good. Ideally, we can come to appreciate that *life is sacramental* in that it manifests the sacred and beckons us to seek and savor life. Life is a type of Eucharist, a banquet of thanksgiving.

Gratitude brings life into perspective. It lessens the sting of negativity. Even when our loved ones push our buttons, act irresponsibly, and isolate themselves in a bottle, we can be thankful, for they challenge us to deepen our relationship with God.

We can even be grateful for our own infirmities, for strength builds on weakness. It is the eternal Paschal Mystery that suffering and death lead to everlasting peace and life. *Deo Gratias.*

A FATHER'S STORY

"If you would have told me five years ago that I would be grateful for my daughter's excessive drinking, I would have said that you were out of your mind, besides being cruel. Now, I think I know what you would have meant.

"If it weren't for my daughter getting seriously out of bounds with alcohol, I might not have come to be the man I am today. I am stronger, freer, and more serene than ever before, and the main reason is that I had to deepen my spiritual life. My difficulties pressured me to purge my old self-sufficiency and religious arrogance, and come to a personal relationship with my God.

"To be sure, I wish my conversion would have happened differently, that my daughter would not have messed up her life as well as the lives of others. But perhaps my daughter's troubles were my opportunities.

"I hope one day my daughter discovers this same kind of relationship with God. I hope she finds true freedom and fulfillment. I hope she gets sober, but no matter what, I will always love her. I could never verbalize and act on such unconditional love before. For these and other experiences, I am grateful."

We can be grateful not only for God and God's gifts but also for others. In the middle of turmoil, we can forget or take for granted people who are there for us: we can be thankful for them now. We can be thankful even for people who enable negative behavior, for their misguided concerns and errors that challenge us to seek the truth. We can also appreciate those who see through the collusive dance of the alcoholic and co-alcoholic, and help us to change our dance step.

Finally, we can *thank ourselves* for cooperating with God and others in accepting what we cannot change—our loved ones—and for being courageous enough to change ourselves. We can be thankful for having the humility to admit to our imperfections and for modifying them. We can thank God, ourselves, and others for not giving up and for finding a better life.

Chapter Fifteen

WHEN YOU FEEL UPSET, HALT

"God, I don't know what to do. It seems like the more I do, the worse it gets. I tried everything, but still the same old, same old. The merry-go-round never stops, and I end up in the same place, dizzier than ever.

"I have to admit he knows how to push my buttons. It irritates me when he looks so calm and I'm so out of sorts. It grinds me when he snores away and I'm awake worrying. I'm ready to jump out of my skin when I watch him comfortably fade away after his third drink.

"I've gotten furious and threatened to leave him. I've begged him to stop drinking. I've been at his beck and call, ready to give him what he wants. And I've withdrawn in icy silence. He still drinks. I'm ready to go crazy. What can I do?"

The first thing to do is *nothing*. Before responding, we must pause to remind ourselves that our spiritual relationship with God, self, and others is the core of recovery. We must pause to connect with our Higher Power in order to achieve serene and effective coping. Such a creative pause is often born out of pain—the pain of frustration, of ineffectiveness, of counterproductive enabling and manipulating, of anxiety, loneliness, depression, guilt, and shame. The pain of futility demands to be heard; it states that there is a better way. Pain draws attention to itself; it tells us to slow down, to halt.

HALT is an acronym frequently used in Alcoholics Anonymous, with different words for what the letters stand for, including this well-known version: When an alcoholic or co-alcoholic is going to make a decision, he or she should HALT if they are

Hungry, **A**ngry, **L**onely, or **T**ired. They should fix those problems first, and only then make the decision.

When *we* are distressed with alcoholic or any other dysfunctional behavior, we can use the acronym HALT in our own way as a strategy for finding serenity.

We can—

- *h*alt and *h*over,
- be *a*ware and *a*ttend,
- *l*isten and *l*earn, and then
- *t*hink and *t*ry.

Rather than react with anger, deference, or withdrawal, we are reminded by this acronym to stop reacting (*halt*) and instead to *hover* around our feelings; to stop repressing our feelings, and instead to become *aware* of what is going on inside ourselves and to *attend* to our own needs. With the support, strength, and safety of love for and from God, ourselves, and others, we are better able to take these first two steps and then to *listen* to our feelings and *learn* from them. Finally, on the basis of this inner security, we can then *think* about what we want to *try* to do.

As we have seen, true awareness is not as easy to achieve as we initially assume. Many of us are more inclined to deny, minimize, or rationalize our alcoholic situation. Moving from nonacceptance to acceptance usually involves considerable pain. This is why HALT is a useful tool. When we give ourselves attention, we recognize and validate how we feel. In response to our feelings, we accept rather than reject, care rather than criticize, show love rather than indifference. We attend to our wounded selves before we do anything. Again, we place ourselves in our inner community of love before we think, decide, and act.

This process may sound complicated and a bit drawn out. Actually, with some practice it can become simple and spontaneous. For example, you catch your loved one in a lie. Instead of expressing or repressing your anger, you can settle and center yourself in love. Instead of exploding (or imploding), you can support and strengthen yourself with God and caring people; and then, in this relatively secure and safe position, you can listen to your feelings: in this situation, you might feel insulted, betrayed, manipulated, or mistreated. Instead of expecting the *liar* to restore your dignity and to comfort you, you can dignify and nurture yourself from within yourself. Such inner care heals and strengthens your wounded self and enables you to think clearly and act appropriately. Finally, instead of retaliating or being a victim, you can confront your loved one with detached and compassionate love.

You may think that it is impossible to do this in a matter of seconds. Initially, it will probably be necessary to call "time out" to *halt* and *hover*, be *aware* and *attend*, *listen* and *learn*, and then *think* and *try* to decide on a course of action. Once again, the key is to create a power base of love within yourself so that you need nothing from the offender and consequently can focus on the issue and speak effectively. Eventually, this decision to act out of an inner bonding can actually become automatic!

So when you are hurt, irritated, afraid, or however you feel, you can slow down, affirm, and attend to yourself. You can experience within yourself what you may want from your loved one. Then you can discern the truth of your feelings, take care of yourself, and finally *choose* what to say and do.

For example, when you are aware of shrinking or regressing to the posture of a child, it is time to HALT. Pausing, you can attend to yourself, maintain your adult stand, and act effectively with detached love. Worry, fear, anxiety, anger, sadness, and loneliness can be cues to take care of yourself. You can HALT your reactions of anger, submission, or withdrawal—attach to love within yourself—and *act* effectively.

DON'T REACT—*RESPOND*

Sometimes the best action is no action. There is no law that says you must act immediately. If a teenager demands that you make an immediate decision about going somewhere, you can bide your time, think about it, and give your decision later. Similarly, you need not respond immediately to the incessant and unreasonable demands of the functional alcoholic. You can give yourself the opportunity to talk the matter over with God, yourself, and others. Instead of reacting with anger or submission, you can keep centered and in control.

So the next time your loved one pushes your buttons, pause and give yourself a break. Take care of yourself first. Go to God and trustworthy people. Consult with them. Pray. Share. Listen. *You are not alone, impotent, or helpless!* Instead, you are with others, powerful, and free. Remember to HALT: that "being-with" precedes, directs, and strengthens doing.

Chapter Sixteen

MANAGING STRESS

When you love a troubled and troublesome person, like a drinker, you will experience considerable stress, and often feel provoked to react in ways that are ultimately harmful to both you and the one you love. Let's talk about ways you can manage this stress constructively.

First, it is helpful to remember that no one can "make" us helpless, steal our choices, or force us to react negatively. How you respond to the stressor or drinker is up to you; the kind and amount of stress you experience are at least partly in your control. Saying, "It's his (or her) fault," suggests that retaining your sanity depends upon that person changing. This is simply not true. You have a choice.

Think of four women whose husbands are late for an important event because of drinking:

Woman A blames herself for not communicating clearly, trying to minimize her husband's irresponsibility. Her attitude is to please him and to make peace at almost any cost.

Woman B gets very angry, blaming her husband for not caring and reciting a litany of his past faults. Her attitude is to retaliate and embarrass him.

Woman C withdraws in cold silence while fuming inside. Her attitude is to hurt him with indifference.

Woman D is not surprised; she succinctly expresses her disappointment, maintains her serenity, and, unlike the other women, has a good time at the event.

What makes the difference between the first three women and the fourth is their *attitude*—the intervening variable between the woman and her alcoholic husband (the stressor). The first three women focused on their husbands instead of themselves. Their well-being depended on their husbands' well-being. The fourth woman had no need to change her husband or to retaliate. Her freedom and serenity came from within herself, and not from her husband.

Your *attitude* significantly influences how well you respond to stressful situations, both in how much stress you experience as well as how well you are able to cope with the circumstances themselves. Most people can handle infrequent difficult events like short-term sickness and even a loved one's death. Eventually most of them regain their equilibrium. However, ongoing stress, like living with a drinker, causes far more wear and tear on your physical, mental, social, and spiritual well-being. Thus, it behooves you to be aware of your beliefs and attitudes, particularly ones that center on problems. For instance, if you believe that you can change your loved one, you will experience much more stress than necessary, stress that may become debilitating. And conversely, if you follow healthy attitudes, you will experience less stress and more serenity.

COPING EFFECTIVELY WITH CHRONIC STRESS

There are two keys to coping effectively with an ongoing source of stress—in this case, the one who has a drinking problem. The first is having a *healthy attitude*; the second is learning and using *positive coping strategies*. We have discussed and will continue to explore how our beliefs and attitudes significantly influence how we construe and respond to problems or any reality. On this basis of looking at ourselves and others in healthy ways, we will now discuss effective coping skills.

THE POWER OF SUPPRESSION

Many of us get caught in an "all or nothing" bind when we are in conflict with another person—either we repress or express, and both responses usually cause more harm (both to self and to others) than good. For instance, when repressing your anger (allowing your emotions to build up), you are liable to implode with stress, fatigue, depression, or psychosomatic symptoms. Or if you do express your anger (aka, blow your stack), you will alienate your loved one, provoke an unproductive argument, or hurt him or her. Both repression and expression make it very difficult for you to take effective care of yourself.

Suppression is a far more constructive way to cope. In fact, it is one of the most important psychological adjustments to real or potential stress. Suppression is different from *repression*. For example, when suppressing anger, you affirm your feelings, then *choose* to put them aside for a time, to "unpack" and handle them more constructively later. For instance, when someone is mean to you, feelings of hurt, fear, and anger are probably connected to your needs. If you repress your feelings, you become out of touch with yourself; you also dam up a flood of feelings that will result in distressful consequences.

Unlike repression, suppression honors your feelings and needs, and it enables you to return to them to care for yourself, to share them, and to learn from them. Instead of being preoccupied with your feelings, suppression allows you to focus on and deal with the issue at hand; namely, the drinker's inappropriate behavior.

One of the best ways to maintain a proper focus when talking with your loved one about his or her behavior is a technique called "share and check." Some of us have the need to share and process everything we feel. We almost feel compelled to be understood and accepted, and consequently we persist in processing our feelings. It is as if our well-being depended on having all our feelings validated. More often than not, this is counterproductive.

Instead, it is generally better just to say something once. For example, "Paul, I felt hurt and angry that you went out drinking with your co-workers last night instead of coming home for dinner or at least calling us." Next, wait for a response. If the response is positive, you can share more. For example, if Paul says, "I'm sorry I made you all wait for dinner. If I'm going to be late tonight, I'll be sure to call," you might answer, "I would appreciate that. What happened last night?"

But what if the response is negative? "Oh, give me a break," Paul might say. "I don't go out that often, and I deserve to unwind after a hard day at work. Quit complaining." *If this happens, arguing it further is probably not productive.* Suppress, and decide the next course of action, which is often a time-out until a later and more advantageous time.

As always, remember to pause and connect with your inner community of love before you speak. Being dependent on your Higher Power (and *not* on your loved one) for your well-being strengthens and protects you. This way, you have no expectations and do not *need* to have the other person accept or understand your feelings. Such inner bonding enables you to suppress more easily and effectively.

OTHER WAYS OF COPING WITH STRESS

In addition to choosing effective attitudes and suppressing our thoughts and feelings, there are other ways to manage the chronic stress of distressful behavior.

Anticipation is particularly useful when you are involved with an excessive drinker. Anticipation differs from *expectation*, which often causes more distress. We have seen that expectations are often too tied up with our needs, and consequently bias our perception and cause unnecessary stress. Anticipation, however, involves learning to predict what is likely to occur because of learning from past behavior. By observing patterns of behavior, you have a better idea of how one will behave in similar situations.

For example, if you have observed that your loved one drinks more on weekends than during the week, you can plan accordingly. If you go to a wedding, you can probably predict that he (or she) will drink too much—or, that he may not drink at all, and instead be withdrawn or irritable, and drink later that night or the next day. Anticipating what your problem drinker is likely to do enables you to have alternative plans and to be less distressed. Of course, your loved one is capable of acting differently than you anticipate, but usually he will return to his usual pattern.

Sublimation is another way to cope with stress. This involves investing your energy in activities (unrelated to your loved one's drinking) that are appropriate and perhaps helpful to yourself and others. For instance, instead of venting your frustration and anger on your children or pets, you can "get it out of your system" in physical activity. It is better to clean house, do bills, or jog than to dump your feelings on your loved ones.

Helping others can also be a way to sublimate and to go beyond your stressful self. When you help a person, you help yourself by getting away from your stress and by adding positive experiences to your life. Furthermore, being proactive creates a positive atmosphere, or at least counteracts negative situations. Don't wait until you feel better to do something positive; instead, do good to feel better.

Sharing with friends and with other understanding people can also be a helpful approach. Simply expressing yourself seldom resolves anything, but it often helps in reducing stress, for we feel support and no longer feel alone. Sharing can also be the starting point of learning how to deal with our feelings and how to heal and nurture ourselves.

Sometimes we share exclusively with ourselves and others, and forget our Higher Power. With good will, we try to be self-sufficient. And, the opposite—to share *only* with God—is equally misguided. Do not forget to share with God *and* with self and others. This kind of spiritual connection is key to effective coping and achieving true happiness.

Finally, *humor* can be very helpful in reducing stress and increasing well-being. Humor is healing: It triggers positive physiological changes, engenders a broader perspective, humbles and elevates us, and lightens us up in general. In humor, we loosen up and do not take ourselves so seriously. Humor can also be a safe and appropriate way of being intimate with someone. Some would say that humor is the springboard to God.

But *how* can you find humor in a stressful and sad situation? Step back, look at yourself, and maybe you can smile at your determined effort to do the impossible—*to change your loved one.* Good humor is gentle and kind; it opens up the possibility of changing for the better. Maybe you can chuckle at some of your own past behaviors and be grateful for more effective coping. Remember that an all-compassionate God is watching over us, smiling with love at our well-intentioned (but ineffective) responses and laughing with joy at our successes.

Inserting ourselves in humorous situations can also reduce stress and engender health. This is not an attempt to deny, repress, or avoid our difficulties but rather a free choice to celebrate life. If you ever go to a support group that is involved with alcoholics or other problem people, you will invariably find humor. Initially, their humor may confuse you or turn you off, but in time you will learn, with the help of God and others, how to smile with compassion, to respond to the humorous in yourself and others, and simply to laugh. You can come to see and feel the incongruities of being human and get a glimpse of a place of perpetual peace.

Chapter Seventeen

IS COMMUNICATION POSSIBLE?

Is it possible to communicate with a person who drinks too much? And if so, how do you do it? Indeed, communication with a brain-damaged person is quite different from communicating with a healthy person.

You cannot expect a person who is drinking excessively to hear consistently and accurately, nor to speak relevantly and empathetically. Alcohol causes brain damage that impairs abstract thinking and short-term memory, as well as judgment and emotional expression. Furthermore, drugs, including alcohol, engender self-centeredness and isolation, which clearly disrupt communication. For instance, cognitive and emotional impairment can be noticed when a drinker repeatedly asks you to repeat yourself, or he repeats himself. More subtly, other drinkers seem to respond intelligently, but upon closer scrutiny you can observe that they respond automatically from a set framework. It is as if they are speaking from taped instructions rather than responding to and exploring what is being said. Their preconceived responses give them and others the illusion of control and communication.

Even when drinkers are *not* drinking, it may be difficult for them to listen and respond appropriately. Forgetting and distortions are common with drinkers who are "dry" (refraining from drinking for a time) but not sober. And even if dry alcoholics are able to hear, they may forget as soon as they resume drinking. So what can you do?

HOW TO TALK TO A PROBLEM DRINKER

Do not expect a drinker, functional or otherwise, to hear or to remember accurately what you are saying or have said. Thus, when your loved one is drinking alcoholically, little true communication can occur. Dialogues are minimal; the reality is a series of monologues. You certainly cannot count on anything that is said or promised, for the drinker is likely to forget or distort. With that in mind, these strategies can help:

Avoid drunken conversations

Do not expect anything when there is drinking. Do not take your conversation at that time seriously. Accept that your loved one is incapable of effective communication. This does not mean that all conversations are futile and meaningless, but rather that what is said at that time may or may not be remembered and acted upon. Better communication is more likely when the drinker is dry, even though he or she may not be truly sober. So pick your time carefully.

Avoid the word you

Particularly in contentious or oppositional situations, the word *you* tends to connote judgment and blame, and it often pressures or threatens a person. Thus, the drinker is likely to take a defensive posture by attacking, submitting to, or avoiding what you say. Whatever the response, effective communication fails to occur.

I instead of *you* statements have a better chance of being heard. So, avoid saying:

- "You make me angry."
- "It's your fault I'm so miserable."
- "What's wrong with you?"

It is usually better to say instead things like—

- "I feel angry/miserable when…."

- "I really care what happens with us, so it scares me when...."
- "Life seems to work better when there is no drinking."

Avoid win-or-lose standoffs

Another common obstacle to communication occurs when the "right" party is unable to look at things from the other person's point of view. If this happens, you will get nowhere. The argument will continue until one or both of you acquiesces or becomes silent. *Someone* has to listen and speak differently.

Although there are indeed absolute rights and wrongs, many issues are a matter of seeing things differently, including absolutes. Rather than judge, lecture, or argue, it is invariably better simply to share your experience, strength, and hope about the issue without a need to be heard, affirmed, or followed. For example, you might think what your spouse is thinking or doing is stupid, irresponsible, crazy, or inappropriate. To tell him so, and then to lecture him on what he should do, will probably provoke withdrawal or an argument. A more effective approach is to listen to and repeat back in other words what he or she is saying.

By repeating what the other person is saying, you demonstrate that you understand. Then with internal prayer, you might share what you or someone else did in a similar situation, and how and why it did not help or even made matters worse. Finally, you can share what worked for you. In this way, you can build an atmosphere of security, respect, and openness that increases the likelihood of being heard. Indeed, such responses are grounded in internal security.

But what can you do when the drinker is attacking what *you* say? Instead of attacking back, you can simply say that you and he disagree or see things differently. Instead of needing to be right, listen to the different and perhaps erroneous view. To be sure, you are not condoning it—and you may be right, while the other is dangerously wrong. Nevertheless, a fruitless argument is circumvented, and if you are not heard, some seeds are planted that may grow weeks or even years later. It is better to love than to be right.

Avoid repetition

Some of us share and process our thoughts and feelings to death, assuming that numerous variations of the same issue will make the other understand. If we have to say something twice, we are getting into trouble; saying it three times probably means that we need to be right and need the drinker to hear and do what we say. Then we are in deep trouble.

Say what you want succinctly and clearly just once. Only repeat in different words when asked to do so. If you catch yourself bombarding the other with explanations or flooding him or her with emotions, you probably "need" the drinker (or anyone) to understand, agree, or apologize. Once again, you then empower the other person and weaken yourself.

Instead, stick to the issue or behavior (not motives), and offer the drinker the opportunity to hear you. Aggressive verbalization, passive-aggressive speech, or tense silence are attempts to manipulate and are counterproductive. When the drinker does show genuine interest, share more.

Do not assume that you know what is best for the drinker, which may or may not be true. In any case, pressuring or manipulating someone is not the answer. However, when we HALT, bond with God's community of love, avoid ineffective coping, and share our truth and love, we are more likely to succeed.

And when we are not heard or taken seriously, we can communicate with God, others, and ourselves so that we maintain our serenity regardless of what happens around us. Attaching to and communicating with God and with reliable people enable us to detach with love, decrease our suffering, and increase our freedom and serenity.

Chapter Eighteen

SETTING BOUNDARIES

A boundary is the line where one thing ends and something else begins. It indicates the extent of something—how far and in what direction it goes. For example, if you own property, it has boundaries within which you can do anything within the law. Your neighbor does not have the freedom that you have with your land. For instance, he does not have the right to build or hold an activity on your land without your permission; otherwise, he is trespassing and usurping rights he does not have.

Boundaries are not only relevant to what we have but also to who we are. Setting and maintaining healthy boundaries are an important part of interpersonal relationships. Our boundaries establish who we are and how far and in what way we want another to go. When someone crosses a line without permission, he or she violates your rights as well as assuming rights he or she does not have.

Setting healthy boundaries can be difficult with a functional alcoholic. Without good boundaries, you will suffer unnecessarily and enable the drinker. Boundaries establish where you end and the other begins; when our boundaries are few or weak, we can get enmeshed with our loved one, thereby losing a sense of self. Or, weak boundaries enable the other person to use and even violate us.

Listen to Pam talk about boundaries:

"I used to be the proverbial doormat. After much pain, I discovered that when I laid myself on the ground, I enabled Jim to walk on me. When I learned to stand tall, to set limits, to stop accepting the unacceptable, Jim began to step back and was less likely to go where he was not invited. I, not Jim, took control of my life. I didn't argue with Jim, but he knew I meant business."

To set boundaries, you must pause, step back, bond with your inner love, and act with no need for anything from the drinker. You seize control (of yourself) and choose: you refuse the unacceptable, assert yourself without aggression, reject being violated, and stand firmly on the ground of love. Establishing appropriate boundaries means that you refuse to allow a person to say or do what you do not want. With the power of love from God, self, and others, you can disengage from codependent vulnerability and enmeshment, and engage with boundaries that protect and proclaim your dignity and freedom.

While good boundaries safeguard us from unfair and harmful behavior, unhealthy boundaries fail to protect us. The boundaries of submissive people-pleasers are tenuous and can easily crumble. More aggressive people use their boundaries as a shield when they attack the drinker. Avoidant people use them as a wall to hide behind. Whatever the case, inadequate boundaries impede interpersonal relations.

Healthy boundaries, on the other hand, serve us by preventing manipulation and exploitation. They encourage us to say "no" to inappropriate behavior that allows a person to appropriate us. We reject being used and abused. Boundaries help us to stop enabling persons to violate us. For instance, if a loved one asks you to cover up or lie for him, to act immorally, to buy alcohol, to take care of his consequences, to demean yourself, or to be a victim, he is probably violating your boundaries.

Healthy boundaries reject such inappropriate behavior. Inappropriate means that something is *not* right, fitting, suitable, or proper in regard to your goals and ideals. When people are inappropriate, they take (or appropriate) what is not theirs, or what they are not allowed or invited to do. As its etymology indicates, inappropriate means that I have taken as my own you or what/who you do not want or permit. I try to make you part of me. Rather than entering such collusion, it behooves you (and me as well) to refuse to engage in such toxic dances.

GUARDING YOUR PERSONAL BOUNDARIES

Boundaries are like principles that we hold sacred. When someone crosses your boundaries, he or she violates what is sacred and shows disrespect for your being a daughter or son of God. And when you give up your boundaries, you dishonor yourself. Maintaining appropriate boundaries proclaims that you respect and honor yourself.

Boundaries vary according to the situation and to whom we are relating. You may open up your boundaries with sober and trustworthy friends and let them get close to you. With drinkers, you have to be careful to prevent enabling, enmeshment, collusion, manipulation, and unnecessary pain.

Listen to Regina, who eventually learned to set and keep better boundaries:

"I still shake when I think of how I let Rex play with my mind. It's as if he took permanent residence in the best room of my mind. He would scold and blame me for his behavior, shouting that anyone married to a b**** like me would be driven to drink. Although part of me knew that his accusations were ridiculous, I still felt guilty or at least doubted myself.

"More painful was his blame that shamed me to impotence. His litany of my faults felt overwhelming and diminished me to the point where I felt nakedly scorned, mocked, and demeaned. Out of desperation or hitting bottom, I learned to stop seeing Rex as the source of my worth. I learned with the help of Al-Anon members to validate my own worth and to take care of myself.

"Looking within, I learned to attach to my Higher Power, not to Rex. My internal bonding enabled me to detach from Rex. When he became judgmental or verbally abusive, I simply stated that it was helpful to know what he thought and felt. I said that we saw things differently and refused to argue or diminish. If he continued to attack, I calmly excused myself, stating that I saw no more value to our conversation, and perhaps later would be a better time.

"Rex no longer resides in my mind. The king has been dethroned; he no longer rules me. The queen has rightfully taken reign and has regained her dignity. At last, thank God, I am free and at peace."

With tough and detached love, we can tell others when a line is being crossed. Like Regina, we can ground ourselves in our inner community of love. Within our boundaries of love, we can be empowered, refusing to enable negative behavior and not allowing ourselves to be abused. We know that part of loving ourselves is setting appropriate boundaries in order to reject inappropriate behavior. Remember: what is good for you is also good for the alcoholic.

Knowing our boundaries also means that we know our own limits, that we are not unlimited, that we are not God. Living within appropriate boundaries, we realize that we cannot fix or save our loved one. We also admit that it is unreasonable to expect a person who is restricted within the narrow boundaries of alcoholic drinking to act appropriately.

Our boundaries motivate us to rely on a boundless God who is capable of infinitely more than we are. When we surrender to God, we find that God does for us what we cannot do for ourselves. Such faith includes and goes beyond reason.

Chapter Nineteen

GRIEVING YOUR LOSSES

"I've lost the man I love to alcohol. As melodramatic as this may sound, it's true. I've watched my husband fade away, leaving me alone.

"A thousand years ago when we fell in love, we drank like all the other young people in our crowd. When we got married and started raising a family, I decreased my drinking and Jim increased his, but rarely to the extent that it caused serious problems. I guess I sort of assumed that he would slow down once the kids were out of the house.

"I also assumed that when Jim took an early retirement, life would get better. I thought we'd be closer, like when we first wed. I expected to go out more, to walk and talk more. I dreamed of vacations, of exploring our wonderful planet, of visiting our children and grandchildren, of enjoying and celebrating life. My dreams didn't come true. Instead, Jim drank even more. Alcohol has replaced these adventures—and, me. What a fool I have been.

"Sure we visit our children and grandchildren and take an occasional vacation, but Jim's drinking is really a burden. For instance, I always have to take the initiative and make the plans; I do most of the driving and talking, often to myself. Jim would be content to stay at home, watch television, and drink.

"What a constricted life! Whether at home or on the road, I have to take care of him. Will I ever stop raising children? Will someone ever care for me? I feel cheated, and I'm angry. I worked hard all my life and I looked forward to my senior years. Instead I feel so used, so tired, so lonely. I'm married and alone. At least if I were a true widow, I'd have more freedom. I get the terrible feeling that I'm going to die caring for people, and no one will care for me."

Carol's story is common. She's fifty-eight and her life isn't over yet, of course. She may live for another thirty to forty years—about half of her adult life. Understandably, she feels mad and sad, trapped, and with little vision of a free and joyful future. Her dreams of harvesting and enjoying the fruits of her toils have been shattered with the reality of caring for a functional alcoholic.

Maybe you can relate to Carol's story. Do you have dreams that you are afraid are never going to materialize? Are your dreams fading away? If so, it may be time to mourn the dream.

MOURN THE DREAM

The *good* news is that Carol is ready to face reality. In the past she may have minimized and rationalized her husband's drinking; now she is ready to face it. But how? And how will *you* do it?

Accept how you feel. Perhaps you feel the way that Carol feels. She's disillusioned and angry at her husband and probably at herself. Hopefully, she will allow herself to listen to, and journey through, her desert of anger and depression and arrive in the land of acceptance.

Acceptance is necessary for effective change. But in order to reach acceptance, we must first work through feelings like fear, anxiety, anger, resentment, and depression. So, in this sense, it is *good* to feel the way we do. Instead of denying, numbing, escaping, or fixating on our feelings, we can come to *accept* them.

To accept that life has been unfair and painful, and that it has not worked out the way we wanted is difficult but necessary—for then we can begin to change the way we cope, as well as modify our dreams. With or without our loved one, we have to seek a better life, the best gift we can give to our families, ourselves, and God.

Determine to change what you can. Pain can motivate us to restructure our lives, to find new opportunities for learning and enjoyment. We can get out and explore what the world has to offer and what we can give in return. For instance, we might explore charitable and enrichment programs in our church, community, and social organizations.

Rather than focusing on our alcoholic drinker, we can detach with love and pursue ways to nurture ourselves. We might make some new friends and take up new hobbies and interests, such as education, reading, physical activity, and travel. For instance, increasingly more people in their forties, fifties, and older are pursing graduate education. If we open ourselves to the changes we *can* make, we can live an infinitely better life.

Deepen your spiritual life. If we deepen our spiritual lives, we will be better able to respond to the joys of an inner journey where God's gifts are experienced. We will learn to recognize and appreciate God's presence within and around us. As we do, new and even better experiences will emerge, ones that will help us cope with our drinker's needy isolation. In this way, his or her problems can motivate us to achieve a better life.

We might discern in the end that God is inspiring us to leave the situation for the good of all concerned. Although we once preferred to share the culmination of our life with the alcoholic drinker, we can accept our loss with sadness and serenity, and continue—perhaps with a hole in our soul—to be fully alive. With or without our loved one, we can explore new possibilities and follow new dreams.

"ONE DAY SHE LEFT AND DIDN'T RETURN"

"It was very difficult for me to come to accept that my wife was an alcoholic. Even when she came home drunk or would be suddenly missing for days, abandoning me and the kids, I would bend over backward to understand and rationalize her behavior. She would blame us for how she acted, and in return we would try to give her what she wanted. We kind of thought that if we were good enough, she would stop drinking and be a good mother and wife.

"Well, one day she left and didn't return. It was sad and scary, but in a way it was a relief. Although my three teenagers had problems, we didn't have to walk on eggshells any longer. We realized how much our lives were centered on her. Her absence forced us to focus on ourselves and start to take responsibility for living the life that God intended.

"In time, we turned our lives around. We all joined support groups, and, with the exception of my seventeen-year-old, we became more active in church. My nonreligious son calls himself a 'reverent agnostic,' and that's okay as long as he keeps searching. As young adults, my kids have come to experience a new freedom, security, and happiness, even though they mourn the absence of their mother. Our family dreams were shattered—and that's unfair. Yet we dream again, more freely and realistically. I am proud of them, and I am grateful for this new life."

Are such scenarios unrealistic? Are such promises illusions? *No!* If you are in a situation like this, you can unlock your shackles and come to a freer and richer life. This is not a false promise; it *can* and *does* happen. The *key is to deepen your spiritual life.*

Still, at times, you will be lonely, sad, and afraid; however, the duration of these emotions will decrease and your strength will increase. You will no longer *need* your loved one in order to be healthy and happy yourself. You will experience a new freedom, peace, and joy that no one can take from you. You may even connect with a healthy person who loves you. These are *not* extravagant promises. You *will* achieve them when you trust God, yourself, and good people.

Chapter Twenty

LIVING WITH A TEENAGED DRINKER

"My son's school counselor encouraged me to go to a 12-step meeting for parents of teenaged alcohol and drug abusers. The first few months were really something. I was so frustrated and angry, actually furious, and yet the other parents didn't get shook up; in fact, they really understood like nobody else ever did. What a relief!

"Some smiled with compassion when I told them how I would check up on my two sons, search their rooms, look for them at night, worry myself sick, and how I would beg, bribe, threaten, scream, and cry. I knew they (the 12-step parents) understood where I was coming from. When I broke down sobbing, they didn't try to silence or rescue me, but they supported me and understood my fears. I no longer felt alone on a drifting boat going nowhere; there were seasoned travelers on the voyage with me, and we seemed to have some direction.

"They helped me make sense of my chaos. I knew that I could trust them. Instead of telling me what to do, they simply shared what helped and didn't help them when they were in similar situations. Some had a son or daughter around my sons' ages; some had children who were younger, and some had adult children. A few, like me, had more than one kid involved with alcohol or other drugs.

"These 12-step parents would also share useful information about the legal system, rehabs, schools, and literature, but most of all they shared their experience, strength, and hope. I took a crash course in addiction and coaddiction, and kept on going to meetings. For the first time in a long time, I felt hopeful and at home.

"I finally realized that I could *not* fix my sons. Actually, the more I tried, the worse things got. I eventually learned that the focus had to be on *me*—the only person I could change. I came to believe that my attitude was the paintbrush of my mind, that it could color any situation.

"I never left a meeting without learning something, because I wanted what the veterans had—serenity, strength, compassion, freedom, happiness. It amazed me that they had found a better life even when their kids continued to use. Somehow it worked for them; maybe it would work for me. That impressed me. Initially I was skeptical about becoming dependent on a program, but I found that I became freer and more autonomous.

"My sons have not stopped drinking completely and have not gotten sober. To watch their lives go down the drain, while their peers who weren't nearly as intelligent and gifted go on to succeed, tears my heart in half. Throughout the last twenty years, they've been on a roller coaster—several times they quit and started to become sons who were open, honest, and touchable. Then they'd start to drink again.

"Sometimes one would get dry and begin to get sober, while the other was using. At other times, both were abstinent, or both were drinking. The scenario never stayed the same for very long. To have expectations was foolish. I learned to always be ready for anything. One thing for sure: life was never boring. Maybe that's the best my sons can do. I hope not. But if it is their best, I'll accept it.

"So why have I continued to go to meetings? I go because of the people and the program; they help me live a better life. My well-being no longer depends on my sons—and that is better for them. I have gained the serenity that I witnessed in my first meeting, which I thought was impossible for me. Hopefully, I can give back some of what was given to me. Maybe I can help some lost and suffering people find direction and serenity."

If you are struggling to love an addicted child, there *is* hope for you. Like this woman, you too can find a fellowship of kindred people, who can help you to learn the principles you need to find a way out of your personal hell.

Adolescent alcohol and other drug problems are especially difficult because they differ from those of adults. Normal changes that take place during adolescence can be intensified and damaged by the presence of a substance abuse problem. When anyone you love is addicted, you will suffer. And when that person is your child, particularly an adolescent, your life becomes a nightmare. To watch your child miss opportunities, fall behind, and lose his or her soul is agony. Dreams disappear. Despair diminishes hope. Life dies.

Listen to a mother whose daughter has a problem with alcohol:

"I just don't understand. What happened to her? What did I do? She was an A student, had nice friends, went to church, got along with my husband and me. We were close. Now she is a D student, has dropped out of everything, has weird friends, dresses differently, has body piercings, and her attitude is godless, oppositional, and distant. I just don't understand it.

"Her guidance counselor tried to tell us that our daughter was probably using drugs. Initially, I reasoned that she was undergoing an identity crisis that would eventually resolve itself. But things got worse.

"I blamed myself for being too strict, and then too lenient. Then, my husband and I blamed each other. It almost destroyed our marriage. I tried everything. I pleaded, bribed, threatened, gave ultimatums, punished, rewarded, withdrew. I'm ashamed of how angry I got. Eventually, I became exhausted and depressed, and finally felt helpless. Our dreams disappeared. I was scared. Would my daughter ever come back? What would happen to her? Would she die? We felt so powerless."

The good news is that in the middle of darkness there is a glimmer of light. Although we have less power that we would like, we are not helpless. It is possible to help our loved ones in their battle with drugs. Much of the rest of this book will handle this issue. For now, here is the rest of this mother's story:

"With the help of addiction counselors, friends, and God, we came to accept that our daughter initially had a serious problem with alcohol and later heroin. When we couldn't accept this fact, things got worse. However, with the grace of God, we learned to accept and manage this terrible reality.

"We learned to love differently, to deal with our pain, to set appropriate boundaries, and to stop enabling. We learned that the only people we could change are ourselves, and this was critical in helping our daughter. We learned how to achieve serenity regardless of what our daughter did.

"To make a long story short, after much suffering, our daughter entered her fourth treatment center, finally got her GED, and is slowly becoming sober. Our daughter who was dead is returning to life. But even if she returns to the dead, we will go on living a good life. This is the best gift we can give to ourselves, to others, and especially to our daughter."

The suggestions that have already been given for helping yourself and your loved one can be practiced with the teenaged alcoholic and/or drug abuser. However, because there is a unique relationship between you and your child, different feelings and problems arise that call for different, additional responses.

We have indicated that an adolescent undergoes many new experiences. New feelings, including sexual ones, emerge, and old emotions are felt in new ways. Interpersonal relations take on new dimensions. Cognitive, moral, and spiritual development goes through several stages. Your teenager's identity is becoming crystallized, often for life. When alcohol or other drugs are added to the mix, your teenager's physiology, psychology, sociality, and spirituality are significantly affected.

Drug abuse retards growth. So, if your child began to drink excessively in early adolescence, his or her psychological and spiritual growth in these formative areas was altered. You have a child who is younger than his or her chronological age. As long as your child is abusing drugs, like alcohol, it is unrealistic to expect him to be reliable, to think clearly, make responsible decisions, or be a mature adolescent. Unlike drinking adults who may still function reasonably well, adolescent drinkers often cannot.

When a spouse or another adult drinks too much, there is fear, anger, depression, stress, confusion, and all the other painful experiences that come with loving someone who drinks too much. But these feelings of pain and helplessness are compounded when it is your child who is losing his or her life to alcohol or other drugs, or both. When you love a child who is hooked on drugs, you are likely to become *more* intense, anxious, and desperate than you might otherwise be.

To watch your adolescent's future slip away, to see the hole he is digging for himself get deeper and deeper, and to feel his deep sense of diminishment can evoke excruciating anguish. It feels like your teenager is dying, and sometimes death might be easier.

Hence, helping your child is very difficult. As one parent said: "I just want to pound sense into him. Doesn't he see how he is destroying his life?" Although the teenager or adult child may have some notion of harming himself, such awareness is repressed and numbed. After all, to admit to self-destruction is a step toward recovery. Although you may try to appeal to the "sane" self in your child, his or her addicted self will fight for its life.

Nevertheless, as a parent we persist in doing what is virtually impossible—to make our child *understand*. We falsely assume that if he understood, he would stop using and get sober. The problem is that we cannot *make* anyone understand—and understanding alone seldom leads to sobriety.

In short, talking in itself—namely, lectures, arguments, pleading, bribing, or loud silence—has limited benefits and often does more harm than good. Particularly with teenagers, actions are far more important than words. For instance, giving consequences for appropriate and inappropriate behaviors is important. Such behaviors as keeping household rules, doing homework, maintaining grades, and doing required chores are the adolescent's responsibilities.

Do not abdicate your power! You can control yourself and what you own, such as your house. For example, your teenager does not own his or her room. Thus, if necessary, check his room for signs of alcohol or other drug use. Do not be intimidated by the ruse that his room is off limits. You are searching it for good reason.

If your child's life is falling apart—like poor grades or high absenteeism, withdrawal and isolation, oppositional and argumentative behavior, dressing and speaking differently, new and shady friends, or however else your child is no longer the child you once knew—you might have to take drastic action. You might have to get the police involved if laws are broken, or you might have to tell your child he or she can no longer live in your house if the drug behavior continues. Such radical action is unfortunate but may be necessary to save his or her life.

Such proactive love is very tough. Much courage is needed. We must be willing and able to withstand our child's vehement protests to the point of being hated. Remember, you are threatening to take from him his source of comfort and fun—and the addict in him will fight back. You must take whatever action is needed; otherwise, your daughter or son may die.

The most important but not the only action is to take good care of yourself. You must achieve and maintain well-being regardless of what your child does. As we have seen, true health comes primarily from within you, not from your child's sobriety. You should want but not need your child to be healthy. Such self-love takes an added burden off your child, and enables you to help him or her better.

Listen to the story of one more parent, who found hope despite her daughter's drinking problem:

"When our daughter had a serious drinking and marijuana problem, I initially denied it, made excuses, and bailed her out of school and legal problems. Oh, how I remember! Often Claire would not come home at night. I would be out all night looking for her, and criticize my husband when he didn't join me. I was always worried and couldn't sleep. I was a mess.

"I would check up on our daughter, go through her things, listen in on phone conversations, follow her, bribe and threaten her, and ultimately scream and be nasty. I didn't like myself. My life was out of control.

"I joined Families Anonymous, a group of parents who had daughters and sons like my daughter, and they showed me a different way. I learned that I couldn't control or change my daughter, but I could change myself. So I began to focus on my needs, beliefs, expectations, and feelings, as well as how to take care of them.

"However, initially I had a problem with the 12 steps that emphasized a Higher Power that most members called God. I had given up on religion and its God a long time ago in college. With patience and acceptance, the members assured me that spirituality need not be the same as religion and that my Higher Power could be anything that was part of or beyond me. Eventually, I came to believe that a Higher Power *could* empower me to cope effectively. Now I am a searching agnostic. Maybe there is a God.

"In short, I learned to take care of myself and rely on the care and guidance of my Higher Power and others. I became stronger and could detach with love when my daughter provoked my anger, and I could connect with others when I felt anxious and afraid.

"I learned to care without worrying, to lessen my frustration, and to be assertive without rage. With gratitude, I learned to regain control of my life. I never thought it was possible to be free and find inner peace regardless of what my daughter or anyone did. But it happened. Thank God? Maybe."

Without the support and help of others, it is very difficult to recover from codependence, especially when the substance abuser is your child. Fortunately, groups like Al-Anon and Families Anonymous are responding to the needs of parents whose children are substance abusers. In fact, some Al-Anon groups are forming subgroups that help caretakers of addicted children. You can locate these groups in telephone books and on the Internet. It is wise to connect with them.

We have seen that it is an agonizing and harrowing experience when your child becomes addicted to alcohol or other drugs. To watch your child or children miss opportunities, seriously hurt their present and future lives, and fall far behind their peers is very painful. To watch your daughter or son evaporate can suck the life out of you. However, when you feel the presence of despair, remember that there is always hope.

Although you can suspend your expectations and dreams, *you must not give up hope!* Like the woman in our examples and the many other men and women, you can survive and even thrive with, in, and through your Higher Power. You can bring God's love to your teenager whether he or she gets sober or not. There is no greater gift.

Only faith in a boundless God can give us boundless life.

Chapter Twenty-One

A FAMILY PROBLEM

When *one* family member has a drinking problem, all the others suffer. Since we are integral members of the same family system, when one member is disordered, the other members must adjust. It is *how* you adjust—and how your children, extended family members, and other loved ones adjust—to the problem drinker's behavior that is the critical issue.

WHAT DO WE TELL THE CHILDREN?

What do you tell your children when their Mommy or Daddy, older brother or sister, grandparent, or anyone they love drinks too much? Actually, the straightforward approach is usually best.

First of all, they probably already know that something is not right. Children are often more observant than we realize. Depending on their cognitive and personal development, which is a function of age and other factors, they will vary in their ability to verbalize their concerns. Nevertheless, they probably "feel" that something bad or unacceptable is going on.

As always, start with recognizing your own problems. If you are in denial or colluding with other family members, then your children, especially the preadolescent ones, will join the game of pretense, repress their feelings, and distort what they see. They can learn to think that drinking excessively is normal and carry (and perhaps follow) these distortions into adulthood.

When you can cope effectively with the drinker, you are better able to deal with and help your children. Before giving them any advice, listen to and understand how they feel, what they know, and what they are doing about it. Validate the truth in what they say, and let them know that they are not alone, that you will always be there for them. Since all your children will experience the same situation differently, each one has to be dealt with both individually and as a family member.

You can tell your children that their loved one has a problem with drinking or that he or she is ill or has a disease. You can affirm that the drinker loves them, but that at times he or she has difficulty showing it, or may act in ways that seem contrary to love. Such baffling and painful behavior can occur even when there is no obvious evidence of alcohol abuse.

Since young children tend to view the world with themselves at the center, they often feel guilty or responsible for things that are obviously out of their control. For instance, children may feel that their so-called bad or imperfect behavior is the cause of their parents' alcoholism or bad behavior. In fact, it is not uncommon for adults to operate according to such childhood standards. Thus, it is very important to clearly state that they are not responsible for their loved one's alcoholic behavior, that they did *not* cause it, nor can they change it.

Nonjudgmental acceptance and understanding will help your children not to feel alone, confused, and afraid. This is the kind of support they need most. Be sure that they know that they can always come to you to ask any question, to get support, to seek protection, to ask for help. Especially if the loved one is abusive, your children should always be able to contact you or some trustworthy person. Sometimes it may be necessary to have an escape plan: a nearby friend or relative whose house your children can run to if they feel unsafe.

As much as possible, help your children to normalize their lives. Besides helping them deal with the negative aspects of family life, offer them opportunities for the positive experiences associated with childhood. With or without the drinker, continue to help them be responsible for learning in school and for their chores. Most important is to be a healthy role model—to walk your talk. To do this, *you must take care of yourself.*

WHEN A SIBLING HAS A DRINKING PROBLEM

What happens when a teenager is in serious trouble with alcohol and/or other drugs, and there are other children at home? Often they know sooner and are better informed about what is happening than their parents are. Your first goal remains the same: to be solid, strong, and serene yourself, so that you may deal effectively with your teenaged drinker. A group like Alateen often helps teenagers deal with the drinking of a family member. In addition, here are some other factors to consider:

Be careful to balance the needs of your other children with those of the problem drinker. Since problem children demand a lot of attention, children who are more quiet and sensitive, or simply better behaved, can become lost or be taken for granted. It is important not to invest most of your energy in your "problem child" and forget about your other children. This can easily happen.

Don't forget to nurture your marital bond. Serious family problems can test the resilience of any marriage. Marital partners often have different styles of dealing with the recalcitrant teen: One parent may be actively confrontational, and the other more passive, detached, or pleasing.

How you handle these parental differences is more important than the fact that the differences exist. You will grow stronger as a couple if you are able to respect and learn from each other's differences, rather than trying to make the other be like yourself.

Secondly when forces outside your marriage are trying to pull you apart, it's important to strive for unity. Unfortunately, instead of being on the same page, many couples are in entirely different books. Then, the drinker will provoke more division and play one against the other. This does not mean that your teenaged drinker is an evil person; it simply means that he or she does what drinkers do.

Ideally, struggling family members can join together in prayer for one another. If this is not possible, then you pray alone. Pray for yourself, for your troubled teen, for your spouse, for your other children. Pray—and God will help you.

Is such spiritual advice pious nonsense, delusional thinking, childish ideation, or an irrational illusion? No, I don't think so. Contemporary science offers an abundance of evidence to support the existence of a Higher Power that is part of and beyond individuals. Call this power what/who you will. But, please, connect with your Higher Power. Such surrender will enable you to achieve serenity and freedom.

Chapter Twenty-Two

WHEN YOU FEEL GUILTY AND WORRIED

When in the throes of trying to love someone who loves alcohol, it is normal to wonder why this is happening to you. "Why *my* spouse, *my* child, *my* sibling, parent, or friend?" you might ask. "Why *me?*"

- Why does Dad drink so much?
- Why does my sister embarrass herself?
- Why did my son drop out of school?
- Why did my daughter leave home?
- Why does my spouse love alcohol more than me?

You might ask these and similar questions, and get few (if any) answers.

We do not know the reasons why some people have problems with alcohol while others do not. There is probably a multiplicity of factors that causes alcoholism. We *do* know that although we influence others, we cannot cause another to drink alcoholically. We simply do not have that kind of power. It may be that we wish we had such power, for if we can make someone drink, then maybe we can make that person stop. It simply does not work that way. Remember, only your loved one can stop his or her drinking and become sober.

APPROPRIATE VS. INAPPROPRIATE GUILT

It is common to feel guilty for something that is really not your fault. To be sure, guilt in itself is not an inappropriate emo-

WHEN YOU FEEL GUILTY AND WORRIED ✦ 119

tion. There are times our conscience *should* bother us: when we are shaming, demeaning, or inveighing against someone, or when we are being manipulative, unfair, or cruel. Although such behaviors can contribute to alcoholic drinking, they are seldom the root causes of the problem. Still, we can and should feel guilty for wrong behavior.

If you are feeling guilty, try to figure out what is making you feel this way. Listen to your guilt. Learn from it. Resolve to make amends to God and to those you have offended, including yourself. Appropriate guilt can motivate you to improve your life. In contrast, if your guilt is inappropriate, put it firmly out of mind. This kind of condemnation and self-recrimination only serves to obscure issues and divert you from what you really can do. It gets us stuck.

Listen to this woman who was plagued with unhealthy guilt:

> "I wish I knew what I did to make my son drink so much. I've questioned myself over and over. Was I too strict? Was I too lenient? Were my expectations too high? Did he start school too early? Was it television? Did he have the wrong friends? Was it that time I screamed at him, or was it that I spoiled him? I've racked my brain to find what I did wrong. If I only knew, then I could have changed, and maybe Chuck would not be in trouble."

This woman is a perfect—and perfectly bad—example of unhealthy guilt that is based on the false assumption that we have more power and control than we actually have. As we have indicated, children think this way; adults should not. Furthermore, getting mired in guilt distorts thinking, wastes time and energy, is emotionally exhausting, and blocks effective helping. It also tends to make us forget the existence of a loving God. Such guilt is neither healthy nor holy, for it impedes effective coping and obscures the presence of a Higher Power.

THE PROBLEM WITH WORRY

"Will it ever *change*?" you may ask yourself.

Like unhealthy guilt, worry is not a constructive emotion. While false guilt places our focus firmly in the past ("If only…"), worry looks too far ahead ("What if…?"). It causes us to obsess about something we cannot control—the future. However, as the proverbial cliché goes, "Yesterday is gone, and tomorrow is not yet here." We only have *today*, and we can do something only about *today*.

Worry is actually an obsessive concern about the *possibility* of something negative happening to someone.

- What if he drinks too much?
- What if she embarrasses me?
- What if he drinks and drives?
- What if she disappears on vacation?
- What if he doesn't come home?
- What if she doesn't keep her promise?
- What if he's unfaithful to me?
- What if my daughter breaks her curfew?
- What if she gets into trouble?
- What if people talk?
- What if I can't hold it together?
- What if I go to hell?
- *What???*

The litany of "what ifs" is endless. You can drown in a flood of possibilities.

Some people feel that if they do *not* worry, they do not care. Indeed, people who worry do care, but worry is not a good way to care. Worry is a colossal waste of time and energy. And like unhealthy guilt, worry obfuscates, distorts, and exhausts. Worry is a poor investment; the debits invariably exceed the credits.

What can you do if you are a worrier? First, recognize that it is counterproductive and unhealthy. Next, detach from your obsessive concern by deliberately turning to another thought or activity that helps you get your mind on something else. Perhaps a repeated prayer or mantra may encourage you to settle and center yourself in your Higher Power. You might meditate on a truth, and allow yourself to be drawn into your Higher Power. Moreover, surrender yourself and your loved one into the care of God.

If you cannot think of what to say to God, try reading and reflecting on spiritual literature. There are plenty of good spiritual books from religious and philosophical traditions, as well as good 12-step books. Our point is that reflecting on spiritual writings can engender insight, strength, and solace.

TRUST

We cannot know past causes and future results, but we can and do know with certainty that both our loved ones and we ourselves will change. Life will get better or worse, and often a combination of both. To continue to worry or feel guilty about our loved ones does not help. We cannot make life work out for our loved ones the way *we* think is best. Ultimately, life is out of our control, but how we respond to what happens is within our power.

Whatever happens, you can rest assured that God will be there for you. Even if your loved one tragically dies without truly living, God is there for both of you. Hopefully, dying from drinking or other drugs is not the best your loved one can do, but maybe it is.

Even then, there can be a profoundly sad joy because God will take care of your beloved, who will finally be free and live in peace. Until then, our prayer is that our loved ones will stop trying to find heaven "in a bottle" of spirits and come to liberation and equanimity in and through the Holy Spirit.

Chapter Twenty-Three

WHEN YOU FEEL ALONE AND LONELY

Karen talks wistfully about her husband, Bob:

> "Our first few years together were great. We did things together, talked and shared, walked and sat together. I felt cherished. But then we started to raise a family, and Bob got more involved with his work, which included extensive travel. I began to feel like a single parent. When Bob was home, he was always busy doing things, which included spending some time with the kids. I also noticed he was drinking more.
>
> "When Bob did have free time, he would drink. Maybe I understood too well; after all, he was a hard worker, good provider, and father, and I loved him. But he didn't have time for me. When I expressed my concern, he would plead innocence, stating that he was doing the best he could, that he was too tired and needed to relax. Then he'd drink some more, and fade into the fog that made good time sharing impossible.
>
> "We drifted apart, always being civil but rarely intimate. This is not why I got married. I thought I'd grow in love, not out of love. What can I do? How can I love my husband so much, and still feel so lonely?"

AN AFFAIR WITH ALCOHOL

Excessive drinking causes many problems, and probably the most serious one is the destruction of intimacy. The depression and isolation of functional alcoholism simply militate against love, leaving you alone and lonely. And so, to be married to a person who has problems of addiction is a prescription for loneliness. You yearn to be touched, to be understood, to be loved—but those yearnings are not satisfied. The fog of alcohol seriously impedes your facing, seeing, and touching each other. Alcohol hides and numbs our sacred and vulnerable selves without which true intimacy is thwarted.

Does feeling lonely mean that your loved one does not love you? Yes and no. Your loved one most likely loves you, but behaviorally loves alcohol more. His or her affair with alcohol excludes and betrays you. Alcohol abuse fosters isolation and insulation, which significantly impedes true intimacy. In a sense, love is present from afar, there but unattainable. So, what can you do?

With courage, be honest: Do you really *need* him or her to love you for your life to improve? Indeed, this may be your *preference*, but it is not going to happen as long as he or she is drinking excessively. Remember: we all need love, but we can get into serious trouble if we need that love to come from a particular person who is unwilling or unable to love. So our challenge is to seek healthy, safe relationships in which we can give and receive the love we need.

THE BEAUTY OF DETACHMENT

It sometimes happens that the families of functional alcoholics lose contact with friends and extended family. In an effort to keep the problem hidden, they may be tempted to pull away from those whose help they need most. If this has happened to you, is it too late to restore ties to those supportive relationships?

Probably not. However, it may mean letting go of (detaching from) the codependent love you have for the problem drinker in order to attach to healthier relationships. Think of it this way: we are called to renew ourselves, to turn ourselves around to where there is *helpful* love.

Such a conversion means that you may have to reach out and make contact with old acquaintances, as well as explore new situations where people may hold interests and values similar to yours. Church and support groups are often places where we find a community of love. We have to learn to put our eggs in many baskets, not one that is riddled with holes.

AVOIDING COUNTERFEIT LOVES

When disillusioned, lonely, and hurt, some people become desperate for love, affirmation, and comfort. If we grow too desperate in our search for love, we become vulnerable to and may unknowingly invite exploitation. It's as though we are wearing a sign on our backs that flashes: "I desperately need understanding, comfort, support, and love." There are many unscrupulous individuals who can read this message from a mile away, and are only too willing to take advantage of these vulnerable people.

One of the most common of these counterfeit loves is inappropriate sexual intimacy. Those who feel little self-worth often cannot stand being alone and may feel they need the love of "someone special" so badly that almost anyone feels better than no one at all. Such relationships invariably cause more pain and loneliness.

There are many other counterfeit loves. For instance, we can futilely try to make work take the place of love. Work becomes the paramount source of our security, purpose, and meaning in life. Or we may join our loved ones in making alcohol our love. When troubled, we go to the bottle for comfort; when happy, we drink. Whatever the activity, we displace true love of God and people, and consequently become displaced persons.

Instead of looking outside ourselves, we must first look within ourselves for the healing grace of love. To cultivate such love, we must recognize and accept that healthy love is ultimately a gift of God, the Sustaining Source of love. We must learn to see ourselves as God sees us: lovable and precious. Gradually, in this way we come to love ourselves and others. This may sound simple, but in some ways it is the most difficult love to achieve. Many of us feel selfish, wrong, or even sinful when we try to love ourselves. However, it is love that heals our feelings of shame and unworthiness. By loving ourselves as God loves us, we protect ourselves from counterfeit love, including abusive relationships.

LONELINESS: SPRINGBOARD TO LASTING LOVE

Loneliness can be a springboard to God, for it pressures us to reach out beyond ourselves, to be in and within Love. When you are feeling alone, ashamed, or unimportant, acknowledge those feelings. Listen to yourself with reverence, kindness, and compassion. Then turn to God in prayer. Ask God to fill you with love.

Even if you feel abandoned by God, God *is* there. The great spiritual writers consistently proclaim that God can be more present in absence, or that God's apparent absence can be the prelude for a fuller presence. This paradoxical process makes logical sense. Since Uncreated Love, or God, is the source of life, loneliness, desolation, or any such feeling affirms the adumbrated presence of God.

You are never alone. Pray to love and be loved, trusting that God *will* answer. God will not always purge your aloneness and loneliness, but will often lessen the pain to make it more manageable. Remember, God abides in you, and you reside in God.

The truth is that loneliness can be an opportunity to know and care for yourself—and others. Instead of being seduced by the counterfeits of love, loneliness can motivate you to love and be loved by God, self, and others. *Loneliness can be a gift.* When you embrace your loneliness and no one is there for you, you can reach beyond your loved ones to the source of love, to the Loved One, to the Lover, to God.

Chapter Twenty-Four

WHEN YOU FEEL DEPRESSED, FEARFUL, AND ANXIOUS

"I tried everything to get my wife to stop drinking and settle down. Whatever she wanted, I gave her. I came home early. I stopped traveling. I always went out with her. I bought her flowers, gifts, made the meals, cleaned the house, took care of the kids, listened to her, and loved her in every way I could imagine. It was never good enough. She still criticized, complained, and blamed. I never measured up.

"As long as she was content, I was happy. As soon as she was irritable or angry, I wondered what I did wrong. It was like walking through a minefield blindfolded; it was just a matter of time until the next explosion.

"It was like I found myself in a deep hole. The more I tried to get out, the deeper and darker the hole got. Life got dark and heavy. I had to drag myself out of bed; I wondered what was there to get up for? I also ate too much, which made me feel more depressed. I knew things were bad when people at work asked me what was wrong or said that I didn't look good.

"I started to take Prozac, which took the edge off and helped me to manage a bit better. I didn't feel quite as down or worry as much, but life was still the same. I still felt empty and confused.

"Then one day in the dense silence of depression, I heard some enlightening words. Well, I didn't hear them literally, but I felt like it was time to get up, look out, and start moving. Although I was professionally successful, personally I was stuck. I had to find help. I got more active in my church, joined the choir, started to work out in a health club, and went to Al-Anon meetings.

"In short, I learned to stop putting my welfare in my wife's hands. That was unfair to both of us. I learned to stop needing my wife to get sober and to stop trying to change her. I learned to change myself—to find happiness regardless of what my wife did. Now, I'm not sure she was ever capable of giving me what I wanted. No wonder I was depressed.

"This experience taught me how to love myself, and to give and receive love from God and others. Sure, I wish our marriage would have worked, and maybe someday it will. But I'm no longer dependent on that happening. I get sad, but not stuck in the pit. Actually, sad feelings now affirm sad realities, and they motivate me to improve my life. It's amazing. I'm better than I've ever been."

COPING WITH DEPRESSION

We have emphasized that when our well-being depends on a particular person, especially a person with serious problems like functional alcoholism, we will pay a terrible price. We are likely to feel depressed, anxious, and fearful. Perhaps you can identify with these "dark nights." If so, listen to what your depression is saying: that you have experienced significant loss, that you feel helpless, that you do not know what to do. Fortunately, your depression can urge you to seek a better and more fulfilling life. God invites and helps us to face, learn from, and transcend the death of depression to pursue the life of freedom and light.

How can our dark nights of depression lead to light days of joy? Think of it this way: Depression slows you down and beckons you to be still and listen. In depression, you might hear the futility of your codependent ways and feel pressured to behave differently. Repeating the same behaviors and expecting different results *are* depressing. Living in a state of constant inconsistency is depressing. Having your dreams go unfulfilled is depressing. When you are drowning in a sea of disappointment and losses, you can be depressed.

If you continue to think and behave the same way and wait for life to change, it will—but not positively. Life will likely get worse, and you will feel depressed. You will feel like the air of life is being pressed out of you, leaving you tired, listless, disenchanted, heavy, uninterested.

Depression is a disturbing call to think and behave differently. "Movement"—physical, psychosocial, and spiritual—is very important. In spite of and because of how you feel, you must move in different directions and/or renew old effective ways that bring interest, motivation, satisfaction, and in general positive results. You must get involved in ways that inflate rather than deflate your spirit.

The weariness of self-dependence may nudge you to seek the energy of a Higher Power. Hitting bottom can motivate you to look up and out for help. Paradoxically, depression can move you to gain a Power that is greater than what you have relied on. Your depression can be a message that beckons you to connect with God and people who have suffered through, survived, and thrived from being in the dark nights of alcoholism.

COPING WITH FEARFUL DAYS

Along with loneliness and depression, fear and anxiety can also emerge when you love someone who has an ongoing affair with alcohol. It is the rare person who has no fear. And you probably have good reason to be afraid. Fear can be a signal to defend yourself, set better boundaries, avoid exposure to unnecessary pain, and reject unacceptable behavior. As with all feelings, *listen to what your fear is saying*.

Instead of being afraid of fear, ask God and others to help you *learn* from your fears. Remember, "courage is fear saying its prayers."

It's helpful to distinguish between healthy and unhealthy fear. Some valid fears from childhood may be inappropriate to carry over into adulthood. For example, it was appropriate, necessary, and helpful to be afraid of being abandoned or not loved by drinking parents, to fear arguments and fights, to be afraid of being criticized or embarrassed. These fears helped you to survive.

However, if conflict and fear of abandonment cause us to hide or act inappropriately as adults, this prevents us from living up to our God-given potential. As adults, we must learn to manage threatening situations as well as prevent childhood fears from being transferred to the present. *When we feel weaker or smaller than we really are, we are probably regressing to a time when fears were overwhelming.*

Other fears may be centered on unrealistic expectations or false beliefs. So, when we change our thinking, our fears will dissipate. For example, if you expect the alcoholic to be consistent, reliable, and really present, you are likely to live in fear and anxiety.

On the other hand, fears can be realistic and healthy when they signal that we need to pay attention to what is happening. When a loved one is volatile, abusive, or violent, it is only prudent to be afraid and to make arrangements for your safety and that of your family. If your spouse or parent cannot be trusted with your children, you should be afraid if he or she (with goodwill) wants to take your children on a trip. When experience has verified cruel criticism, overspending, drinking and driving, or broken promises, you *should* be afraid.

Healthy fears mobilize our defenses. They move us to stop, think, protect ourselves, and defend against destructive behavior. *Unhealthy fears immobilize and diminish us.* Whether our fears are healthy or unhealthy, realistic or unrealistic, our challenge is to face them with the help of God and understanding people so that we can learn to cope courageously with the realities of our fears.

COPING WITH ANXIETY

It is almost impossible *not* to experience anxiety when you love a functional alcoholic. Although anxiety and fear are similar and are often confused, they do differ. Fear is usually fear of something specific, such as your loved not keeping a promise, avoiding or rejecting you, or causing disruption. Anxiety is more free-floating, amorphous, and less definitive.

When you are anxious, you feel like you are standing on shaky ground, uneasy and uncertain, and in disharmony with yourself. You are likely to feel anxious when you do not know where you stand and what is going to happen.

Anxiety often indicates that our identity is changing or is under the threat of change. For instance, if you see yourself as a fixer—that your good behavior will fix your loved one—your identity and life can be shaken to their foundation when he or she gets worse. If your identity excludes anger so that you repress anger, you will feel anxious when you are angry.

Instead of getting anxious about *being* anxious, you can be aware of, accept, listen to, and learn from your anxious self. Place yourself in the presence of caring people, and ask God to help you become more comfortable with the situation.

Listen to your anxious self; it is telling you that there is another and better way—that you cannot change your loved ones but can accept and cope with them in more effective and serene ways. Your anxiety beckons you to look clearly and dearly at the painful realities and to listen to your repressed feelings. Always do this processing with God, and, when feasible, with helpful people.

Anxiety can also be the consequence of *healthy* change. For example, when you begin to love yourself as much as the problem drinker, you may feel uneasy about it, as if it were wrong or unnatural. You may feel uneasy about setting boundaries, refusing to accept unacceptable behavior, or doing something good for yourself regardless of what your loved one does. Moving from codependency to autonomy may initially evoke anxiety. It is important that you sometimes act contrary to your feelings. Eventually, you *will* become more secure and serene.

Rather than being anxious about being anxious, embrace your anxious self. Standing on the precarious ground of anxiety, you can break through to a more secure and stronger place. When you connect with God's community of love, your anxious self will be comforted, assured, and strengthened. You will learn how to rest in the eye of a storm.

No matter what, you can learn to feel serene in the security of your Higher Power, or, in love. Seldom do we change significantly without taking such a leap of faith. Existential anxiety is the beginning of this fundamental option.

Chapter Twenty-Five

RESTORING BROKEN TRUST

"It all started when I found out that our utilities were going to be shut off because the bills had not been paid. Dummy me, I assumed that my husband was taking care of the bills. That's what we agreed to. When I confronted him, he sheepishly admitted it, stating that he planned to pay them. Then I discovered that our credit cards were almost maxed-out. When I asked him about that, he just said he didn't want to worry me.

"Where is all our money going? I asked him. He just looked at me like a deer frozen in a spotlight, and said he didn't know. But as we took a closer look at the bills, the truth came out: his twenty-dollar lunches, after-work bar bills, and his fully stocked basement bar. Here I am, tightening my belt to save, and he is spending like a freaking millionaire.

"What upset me most was that I had been deceived. He lied about everything. I trusted him, and I feel like I've been taken for a ride, that I've been used. I feel like a fool. I suppose I'm also mad at myself for having my head in the sand. It will be a long time until I trust him again. I'm not sure if I ever will. I love my husband, but without trust, what kind of a marriage can we have?"

You really cannot trust a person who loves a substance (or activity) more than he or she loves you. Sooner or later, you will be disappointed and probably, like this woman, be very hurt. Not all alcoholics are as irresponsible as this woman's husband. Some drinkers can be trusted to function well in their work and to be responsible with household duties. Most alcoholics, however, will not or cannot be consistently reliable. One day they act responsibly, and the next day they let you down. You never know who is going to show up. Such is the nature of drinking alcoholically.

To learn to trust intimately again is a more difficult and important matter. To trust enough to risk sharing your wounded and vulnerable self takes time. With or without your problem person, you need to heal and gain the strength to be openly in love again.

But if drinking progresses, problems proliferate. The need to cover up and gain control increases. Drinkers become more and more irresponsible, dishonest, and devious in word and deed. Their love of alcohol will have a negative effect on their thinking, decisions, feelings, and behavior. As drinking increases, the more untrustworthy he or she is likely to be.

LEARNING TO TRUST AGAIN

Listen to this parent:

"Even though our daughter did well in her month stay at the rehab, and even though she's been sober and has been going to meetings for the last six months, we don't fully trust her. Even though our old responsible daughter has reappeared, we're still leery of her. When she says she's going to a certain place, with certain people, and will be at home at a certain time, I say to myself: We'll see, uh-huh, maybe. When I see her happy, I wonder if she's been drinking or taking some other drug. When she's irritable, I wonder if she's coming down from something.

"I don't always believe her, even though there's no overt reason to doubt her. It's kind of unfair to her, yet in light of her past, it is understandable that we can't naturally trust her. It used to be that we knew our daughter was lying whenever she moved her lips. Well, it's not that bad now, but I'm afraid that it's going to take a long time before we really trust her. Deep wounds take a long time to heal. And if they do, scar tissue will remind me of painful times."

Indeed, deep wounds take considerable time to heal, and they always leave a scar—a sign of woundedness. And although you cannot control the healing process, here are some ways you can help it.

To be sure, we cannot force anyone to trust and be trustworthy. Sometimes trust and love are renewed—and sometimes they are not. Regardless of what happens, as usual, you begin with yourself.

You may have reason to distrust yourself. If what you have been doing is not working, your pain can lead you to pause, pray, reevaluate your approach, and get help. You can own up to your distrust of your thinking, decisions, and behavior, and hand them over to God.

Then, you can try to trust others who have been where you are and have made it through. Such trustworthy people can support and comfort you. They can also guide you to avoid foolish decisions and actions, as well as to make wise ones. Because of better coping, you will learn to trust yourself.

Indeed, it is paramount to trust God. When you rely on your inner community of love, you learn to listen, think, decide, and act more effectively, even in the middle of a drinking situation. Standing in love frees you from needing your loved one to be trustworthy and enables you to accept and manage whatever happens.

Such transformative trust is not easy. Many of us cannot or do not want to let go of our control and let God be in control. It is challenging to trust that God knows and will help you to act appropriately. To surrender to God's will means to put your self-will aside and allow God's way to be manifested in yourself, in others, and in God's Spirit and Word.

Then, as you grow in knowledge, strength, and freedom, you will learn to trust yourself to choose and act effectively for yourself and others. You can give your loved one chances to succeed and fail at trust, and be willing and able to handle the consequences. You will be able to cope with the drinker's unreliability, denials, and sneakiness. In spite of distrust, you will still hope for a better day.

If you and your alcoholic are becoming sober, you will grow in trust. Your loved one will eventually become trustworthy. However, it behooves you to avoid rash judgment and remain open when old feelings reemerge. When something evokes distrust, wait for conclusive evidence before you speak. Until then, trust yourself and God.

This woman describes the typical difficulty in trusting a recovering alcoholic:

"It's been three years since my husband started walking on the road of recovery. He's returned to the man I wanted to marry, and life is closer to what I dreamed of.

"I hasten to add that I still go to two or three Al-Anon meetings per week. I try to give back some of what I received. And I periodically experience bursts of worry and anxious distrust. This is humbling, for it lets me know that I am still in recovery myself. Oddly enough, I am grateful, for my imperfections keep me growing.

"Here's an example of what I mean. Last week, Jim told me he would meet me after work for dinner at 6:30 p.m. As usual, I was a bit early and arrived at 6:15. At 6:37, Jim had not arrived. Seemingly out of nowhere, I felt feelings I had five years ago—worry, blame, anger. There he goes again, I thought. I knew it wouldn't last. Just wait when I see him. A litany of faults flashed in front of my mind's eye.

"Then I caught myself slipping back to old thinking. I turned to my Higher Power, detached from my stinking thinking, and let go and let God. I regained most of my serenity. At 6:41, Jim showed up, apologized, and explained why he was late. He had a perfectly valid excuse. The wrongdoing was on me, not him. But I didn't get trapped in old habits; so we had a wonderful dinner."

No matter what happens, always pray to trust that God cares for you and your loved ones. It takes trust to turn our will and lives over to the care of God. When we can let God be in the center of our world, a burden is lifted. We are comforted and can rest in some peace in knowing that God is taking care of us.

Chapter Twenty-Six

LEARNING TO CARE
FOR YOURSELF

Wife of a functional alcoholic for thirty years, a woman was given a "homework assignment" in counseling. She was to do something unnecessary and frivolous for herself. The following week she reported that it had been one of the most difficult assignments that she ever had. She explained that she had always bought something for herself only when she needed it. When she did recreate, it was always with and usually in service of someone else. Finally, she said she bought herself an ice-cream cone. She said that she felt almost guilty eating it, and she kept looking for someone to share it with.

Like this woman, the longer you are ensnared in the cycle of codependency, the deeper the wounds and the longer those wounds take to heal. You can forget, or may have never learned, how to care for your own health. And when you do begin to change your ways, normal actions of self-caring can feel unnatural or selfish; they can even evoke guilt. But when you fail to take care of yourself, life gets worse for everyone, including your excessive drinker. For instance, you will become less capable of coping with and helping your loved ones. When this happens, you can also forget God, who wants what is best for you.

So how should you care for your own health?

WATCH YOUR THOUGHTS

Abstain from thoughts and behavior that harm you and enable problem drinking. This involves first becoming aware of your false beliefs, unrealistic expectations, unnecessary fears, needy and enabling behavior, and overt and covert manipulation. It is only then that you will be able to change them.

GET HELP

Learn from knowledgeable people about problem drinkers and those who love them. Join a 12-step group. Hopefully, reading this book is a good start. Remember to bond with God and God's community of love that dwells within you.

PRACTICE EMPOWERING BEHAVIORS

Connecting with God's Spirit empowers you to practice proactive attitudes and behaviors like detached love and boundary setting. Learn to grow from your painful times. Instead of avoiding, numbing, repressing, fighting, or exacerbating your unsettled feelings, you can learn to listen to their message and become stronger. With God and helpful people, so-called bad times can lead to better times.

PRAY EVERY DAY

Begin each day with an affirmative, proactive prayer that orients you to cope and to live as well as you can. One man begins his day by saying "Yes!" to life and its possibilities, thanking God for life's gifts, and affirming for himself that he is never alone. His first words of a new day are, "Yes, we thank you."

Whatever your own prayer is, get in the habit of proclaiming a reason for being that goes beyond the ordinary. For example, try to avoid needing anything from any one person except God. Rely on God as your sustaining source of serenity, not the drinker or anyone else. Bond with God; act as *we*, not *me*. Seek to live a virtuous life, especially one of *love*, no matter what happens. Join or form a community of love. See and respond to the presence of God in everyone.

When a loved one pushes your buttons or hurts you, avoid reacting with anger, withdrawal, or submission. Instead, pause—and bond with God and others on whom you can safely rely and be strengthened. Instead of automatically reacting in ways that only exacerbate the situation, first pause, turn in to the Power that dwells within you, think and access the situation, and then act. The challenge is to maintain your serenity regardless of what is happening. In other words, pray.

STAY IN GOOD PHYSICAL CONDITION

When distressed with problem people and problems, it is easy to indulge to comfort ourselves. We can "over" do it—overeat, oversleep, overwork, overindulge in television, movies, the Internet, and so on. Such methods of lessening stress and comforting ourselves are appropriate in moderation. However, to get too much too often, though commonly done, causes more problems and exacerbates existing ones. Actually, this approach is somewhat similar to what the drinker does. It offers short-term relief—and long-term grief.

Clearly, there are many common but less-than-healthy ways to gain temporary relief but lingering distress. To achieve and maintain good physical condition is very important. Try to get and stay in good physical condition with good nutrition, regular exercise, proper sleep, and healthy habits. Exercise, for example, sublimates and reduces stress, produces pleasurable and healing biochemicals, increases self-esteem, engenders perspective, and fosters overall well-being. Usually, the most important and difficult step of exercise is the first. Once you start, the middle and end will occur with much less effort. In other words, *getting* to the health club, exercise class, or the walk is usually more difficult than the workout itself.

MAINTAIN GOOD "SOUL HEALTH"

Involve yourself consistently in life-affirming activities. Yoga, Tai Chi, Pilates, dance, and other similar practices are increasingly popular ways to relax and reduce stress, to engender serenity, and to evoke healing and wholeness. Such practices are always good and are especially recommended when distressed.

BE PART OF A GROUP

Don't forget to maintain or build support networks. Never underestimate the positive effects of simple friendship, sharing, and humor. In addition to support groups for problem drinkers and their families, consider faith-sharing fellowships, discussion groups, or esthetic, cultural, and athletic events. The important point is that you stay active and build a satisfying life for yourself.

Theoretically, such a program of fostering growth may sound easy, but experientially most people have difficulty. Besides societal factors that militate against health, when you focus too much on caring for problem people, you can forget and abuse yourself. You must decide how to take care of yourself, and not rely on the unreliable people. Your well-being is your responsibility. *Don't forget yourself.*

BE A GOOD STEWARD

Remember that we are stewards of God's gift of life. For many of us, we must turn the Golden Rule around: Instead of doing for others as we would have them do for us, we must learn to love ourselves as well as we love others. As we do these things, we will be better able to help others and to build God's kingdom—to experience less painful fragmentation and more serene oneness.

To that end, we must let God and others love us. This is not easy because we are much better at loving than at being loved. Let us gratefully and joyfully pursue and accept God's gift of life-giving and redemptive love. This power of love protects, consoles, strengthens, directs, and inspires us to seek, seize, and savor the good life.

In the best and worst of times, trust that God empowers, enlightens, liberates, and gives us peace.

Chapter Twenty-Seven

GETTING THE HELP YOU NEED

"Everyone thinks that I'm crazy for thinking my wife has a problem with alcohol. They don't say it, but I feel it. They're thinking, 'She's raised two fine children, keeps an orderly house, is an outstanding high school teacher. How could she be an alcoholic?' But they neither know nor care about her private life; as long as she continues to perform well, they're satisfied. I'm the only one who really knows about her drinking.

"Yet being alone with my convictions, I'm starting to doubt what I see and feel. Maybe I am exaggerating, or maybe I'm not seeing the whole picture. I feel like I'm on a boat all by myself, and no one understands or cares. And waves of alienation and self-doubt are exhausting me. Should I abandon ship?"

The man is *not* alone on this boat; actually, it is quite crowded. People who love a "classic" alcoholic—one who is blatantly disruptive—often receive more sympathy and support than those whose alcoholic is more functional in public. If you love a functional alcoholic, you can easily feel that people do not understand or offer help, and instead they criticize or withdraw from you. As we have seen, as long as the drinker is functioning effectively and is successful, most people deny or do not care about the more personal problems. They collude with one another to deny and rationalize excessive drinking. Nevertheless, you need not stand alone.

Most often, it is the people who are in your situation—families of other problem drinkers—who are probably going to be your best source of support. You need people who really understand what you are going through, who hear what you are saying and feeling, and who do not look at you like you are speaking Martian. Their understanding validates your feelings and liberates you from your isolation and engenders hope.

If the idea of talking to a stranger is too much for you, look closer to home. You may have a maverick relative who has the courage to listen and speak differently. Or perhaps there is a friend, clergy person, or counselor who can help you to make sense out of what is nonsense to most people.

SUPPORT GROUPS

Many people turn to support groups for help. These are groups of people who meet regularly to help one another cope with and care for excessive drinkers. Most of these groups practice what is called a 12-step program of recovery, based on the one originating with Alcoholics Anonymous. Groups like Al-Anon, Families Anonymous, Co-dependents Anonymous, and Adult Children of Alcoholics offer a holistic approach that integrates biomedical, psychosocial, and spiritual principles of recovery within a fellowship of acceptance, understanding, and useful knowledge.

One way to begin is to contact the group's headquarters (via phonebook or Internet) and acquire a list of meetings in your area. Go to at least six different meetings. Also shop around for the meetings where you feel comfortable, because the group at one location may offer a totally different experience from the group at another. Or you may begin with reading. Fortunately, there is a multitude of books explaining the 12-step approach to recovery for drinkers and their loved ones. It is the rare person who would *not* benefit from perusing some Al-Anon literature and attending their meetings.

"12-steppers" are quick to point out that their program is *not* based on any religion because they want *everyone*, regardless of their religious affiliation, to feel welcome. Although the historical foundations of 12-step programs are *rooted* in Christianity, the program itself fosters a deep sense of spirituality without proselytizing for a particular religious tradition.

INDIVIDUAL COUNSELING

You may not feel comfortable with a 12-step group, or you may not feel that they are addressing the needs of less-functional alcoholics than your loved one. If you do not feel at home with 12-step meetings, then it may be worth trying a competent licensed counselor.

If you do decide to go this route, keep in mind that not all professional counselors are trained to help persons who care for problem drinkers. Do not automatically assume that any physician, counselor, or clergy person will be able to help you. Most professionals receive little or no education about helping those who live with alcoholics. If this is the case, even with the best of intentions, they may do more harm than good. Before making an appointment, find out if this person specializes in addiction and especially coaddiction.

Certified drug counselors or social workers who work in drug/alcohol treatment facilities are more likely to understand your real-life situation and can offer useful advice on what to do and where to find more help. In addition, it is not rare for recovering co-alcoholics to be more helpful than professionals, and they do not charge you anything.

INTERVENTIONS

In some cases, a functional alcoholic and that person's family may best be helped through what is called an "intervention." An intervention is a group of caring people who act in concert to directly confront the drinker in order to break through his or her distorted thinking and motivate him or her to seek help. The process involves pointing out, with compassion and detached love that eschews resentments and arguments, specific examples of when your loved one drinks too much, and how his or her behavior affects you. Sometimes the power and care of the group will help to break down the denial, which in turn can lead to a breakthrough to recovery. Such a process can also be used on non-drinking enablers to motivate them to seek help.

It is important to enlist a person who knows how to plan and run an intervention. A reliable resource is often a drug rehabilitation facility. Call a few of them and explain your situation. Or long-time members of Alcoholics Anonymous and Al-Anon often know of people who are competent in conducting an intervention. You can contact such people by calling your local A.A. or Al-Anon headquarters or by going to some A.A. or Al-Anon meetings and asking.

If you decide to execute an intervention *without* the help of a professional mediator, use the principles already discussed, such as avoiding "you" statements and "always" accusations. Hopefully, your compassionate and tough love will encourage the alcoholic to see things differently and to seek help.

REHABILITATION PROGRAMS

Professional treatment programs for people with alcohol and other drug problems are available and are often covered by medical insurance. Such rehabilitation facilities usually offer residential programs as well as outpatient (daily or several times weekly) treatment.

Rehabilitation facilities offer a variety of services, including detoxification (if needed), individual and group counseling, family therapy, 12-step oriented treatment and meetings, structured exercises to increase awareness, didactic instruction, thought-pattern restructuring, and positive habit formation. Such a comprehensive approach is often the drinker's best chance of getting sober.

These recovery programs usually involve the loved ones of the alcoholic. So, regardless of how your loved one responds, *you* can take advantage of the opportunity of learning new ways to care for and help yourself and your loved ones. Participate in any family sessions, talk to the counselors and ask questions, read addiction and codependency literature. No matter what, you can learn new ways to cope and improve your life.

Above all, seek the help of your Higher Power. This does not mean excluding other forms of aid, for God works through people, places, and things. Nor does it mean that if you pray, everything will turn out just the way you want it. Nevertheless, as we have seen, prayer is paramount. Turning yourself and your loved ones over to the care of God *will* help. Putting yourself and them in the presence of God will strengthen, enlighten, console, and protect you and them.

Chapter Twenty-Eight

INDIVIDUAL INTERVENTIONS

Because the family of a functional alcoholic frequently perpetuates the problem through enabling behaviors, it is sometimes the case that the first people to notice the problem are outside the immediate family circle.

John is one such example. Although he likes his brother-in-law Jeff, he is concerned about how Jeff's drinking is affecting his sister and her kids:

"I don't know what to do. My sister gets more and more miserable every day, and all I can do is stand by and do nothing.

"Jeff's a nice enough guy, but he drinks too much. My sister gets stuck with most of the burdens of raising a family and keeping a house. He works, drinks, and plays, and my sister tolerates it. I think he's using her, and I feel I've got to do something. Am I out of bounds?"

Sometimes it is a co-worker who gets involved:

"Joe is a co-worker and a friend, too. Although he meets his quotas, it seems like he drinks more than he should. You know, he has two or three drinks at lunch, gets high at parties and picnics, or comes to work with a hangover. I get the feeling that Joe is on a slippery slope, and I don't know how to get him off. Frankly, I'm not even sure I should try."

WHEN SHOULD YOU SAY SOMETHING?

Almost everyone cares about someone who drinks too much. Whether that person is a spouse, child, sibling, parent, or friend—

an employer, employee, or coworker—the problem may never change unless we summon up the courage to do something.

Like the people in the previous examples, you may wonder what you can do to help. Like them, you may be sensitive to overstepping boundaries, or afraid of hurting or alienating the other person. You may feel powerless to do anything, or afraid of doing more harm than good.

The following man is afraid to say anything to his mother. He is concerned because her drinking has increased since she began living alone after her husband's death.

"How do you tell your sixty-seven-year-old mother that she drinks too much? When I call her, I can tell if she's been drinking. Her speech is measured and slightly slurred; her thinking and recall are not sharp, like they can be in her sober state; and she is emotionally reactive and volatile. She really can't hear what I'm saying or discuss issues, but rather she is on the defensive and is easily hurt. I feel I have to walk on eggshells and monitor everything I say. I want to help my mother, but I'm not sure how to do it. I don't want to hurt her feelings or for her to get mad at me."

In a sense, your ability to help *is* limited. As we have seen, you cannot change, control, or cure *anyone* even if your loved one wants to be helped. Yet when you *accept* and act on the reality that you cannot fix anyone, new possibilities emerge. With your Higher Power, you can also read and read, listen and listen, ask and ask, search and research. You can pursue information and formation about drinking and caring for drinkers from books, articles, and knowledgeable people. Then, you will be in a better position to facilitate change.

TALKING TO THE PROBLEM DRINKER

When dealing with someone with a drinking problem, it is important to abstain from criticism, judgment, and psychological analysis. These approaches usually threaten the drinker, may be insulting, and are often attempts to manipulate.

What you *can* do is to express your concern about your loved one's well-being. If he or she tells you not to worry and that everything is okay, you can succinctly state with compassion what you are concerned about, like his or her unhappiness, irritability, withdrawal, sleeping habits, and drinking too much. Be caring and concrete. Reinforce that you are not trying to criticize but that you are concerned. Focus on *behavior*, not *motives*.

If after a time the drinker begins to listen and wants to hear more, you can talk about available help. It is not likely that this will happen right away, and may never happen at all. Nevertheless, you have accomplished much. You have told your loved one that you are concerned, have given him or her the opportunity to hear you and get help, and probably have planted some seeds that someday may engender growth.

Consider our example of John whose brother-in-law's drinking is causing problems and who is understandably concerned about his sister's welfare. If John has a close relationship with Jeff, talking to his brother-in-law may help, but often such conversation exacerbates the situation. Actually, John's sister could be left with (negative) consequences of his intervention.

John is probably better off meeting with his sister. Rather than initially giving advice, John can invite his sister to share her feelings, while showing compassion and support. He can let her know that she is not alone. Then he can suggest readings and people who have emerged healthy from similar situations. No matter what, John can let his sister know that he will always be there for her.

Or think of the man whose mother drinks; he may say something like this:

> "Mom, what I'm going to say to you may sound like I'm criticizing you. That's not my intent. My concern is that often when I call you, I think that you have been drinking. I know you have said that you just had a drink to take the edge off. But it's tough to communicate with you, and I'm afraid that we're drifting apart. I don't want that to happen.

"Again, my intent is not to beat up on you, but rather to show my concern and offer any help I can give. I don't know if you realize that at family gatherings your drinking gets out of hand. It's not that you embarrass or abuse anyone; it's more like you fade away as the evening gets longer. Even your grandchildren ask what's wrong with Grandma. Anyhow, I just want to let you know that I care and am willing to do anything to help. Whatever happens, always know that I love you."

The last sentence of this man's individual intervention is important. Express your love in your own way and *mean* it. It is quite possible that your loved one will never become permanently sober. Still, it makes a huge difference to him or her to know that you care and are willing to help. Always wait to express your concern until the drinker is not actively drinking and thus is relatively more accessible. Whatever the eventual outcomes, try to avoid enabling behavior, and continue to love and enjoy your loved one as much as you can and as much as your loved one allows.

Individual or group interventions don't always work but are always helpful. In any case, know what you are willing and able to do. Do not make promises you cannot keep. Avoid placing your own well-being in the alcoholic—or, *needing* your loved one to be healthy. Always put yourself and your loved ones in the care and love of healthy people and God. Know that drinkers can, hopefully sooner than later, ultimately find peace and be who God wants them to be.

Chapter Twenty-Nine
MAKING AMENDS

"Make amends?" you might be saying. "Why should *I* make amends? It seems clear that the drinker has caused all the problems."

We have seen that it is not that clear or simple and that we too usually have a hand in the very process that is testing our sanity. That is something we can change. In this sense, it is *good* that you are part of the problem.

How does making amends fit into the picture? Actually, it plays a significant role in coping with your loved one and, more importantly, in achieving your own serenity. What does the process mean?

As its etymology indicates (from the Latin *emendare* = "to free from blemish or fault"), amending your life means that you continually try to free yourself from faults that you work on changing for the better. Making amends indicates goodwill and reparation toward those we have harmed. Amending our ways and making amends engender balance in ourselves and heal relationships. To reconcile, we must have a firm purpose of amendment.

You can make amends by starting with yourself—with how you have hurt yourself. For example, when you are involved with a functional alcoholic, you can easily neglect yourself; thus, you can make amends by taking better care of yourself. If you have beaten yourself up or worried yourself sick, you can stop violating yourself and start to learn healthy ways to treat yourself. You can change negative and catastrophic thinking and behavior to positive and realistic thinking and behavior.

After all, we have the obligation to treat ourselves justly and mercifully. God's love demands this of us. Remember, when you improve yourself, you help your loved one as well.

As mentioned earlier, one of the most stressful situations occurs when one of your children is an alcohol or drug abuser. In such a situation, it is easy to focus too much on your teenaged drinker and neglect your other children. Such behavior is understandable and common, but certainly not right. You can make amends by tuning in to your other children and spending some time with them as a group and individually.

When one of your children is having problems with alcohol and/or other drugs, your marriage is usually severely stressed. It is common to see and act differently than your spouse does, not only to disagree but to argue and perhaps become alienated from each other. *Losing your marriage helps no one.* Marital problems are signals to stop and reassess the situation, and perhaps get professional help.

Once again, the best way to make amends is to improve yourself and hopefully your spouse will do the same. The goal is that your crisis will strengthen and unify your marriage rather than weakening and dissolving it. Unity, though not essential, is very helpful in dealing with a troubled child.

If you have unjustly hurt your spouse, you can express your sorrow, and if possible try to make it up. For example, if you tried to manipulate your spouse (like, "you must do it my way"), you can apologize and make amends. You can halt your control and try to come to a unified stand. You can schedule time and space just to be with each other. You can go out to dinner, the theater, a ballgame—whatever you both enjoy. Although personal wounds take time to heal, they do not heal spontaneously. You must actually *care* for wounded people, most especially yourself.

Making amends to your problem drinker may be more difficult, especially if he or she is *still* drinking. Again: the most basic way to compensate for harm is to improve *yourself*. Instead of trying to control the drinker and expecting your loved one to stop drinking because of your care, you can accept and love the drinker unconditionally. You can stop enabling, detach with love, and continue to keep appropriate boundaries. Letting the drinker have his or her pain rather than increasing or decreasing it can be a way to amend your own ways. You can say you are sorry when you unjustly offend the drinker, and you can try to reconcile.

Above all, you can *pray*, asking God to take care of both of you. Putting your alcoholic in God's care not only helps you to avoid and compensate for your wrongdoings but also allows God to help. Turning your child over to the care of God does *not* mean that you abdicate responsibility. Indeed, you avoid enabling, set boundaries, offer help and opportunities, and let your loved one experience his or her pain, unless unable to care for him- or herself.

Finally, you can make amends to God. We have seen how easy it is to forget God when in the throes of interpersonal pain. If you have turned your back on God, you can turn around and face God. Or if you use God as a consultant, you might try to surrender to God, You can discern and do God's will rather than trying to make God do your will. You and I—all of us—can admit that we have much less power than we thought, and we can turn our life and will over to the care of God.

Chapter Thirty

DRY AND SOBER—
NOW WHAT?

What if your loved one stops drinking? Then what? To be relieved and hopeful is fine. To assume that everything will be all right is foolish. Let us look at some of the possibilities of what can happen when a functional alcoholic stops drinking.

A "DRY DRUNK" IS NOT SOBER

The fact that someone is able to abstain from drinking does *not* mean that he or she is actually sober. In fact, sometimes the real work of sobriety *begins* here, and for some people that means life can get even *more* difficult than when that person was drinking. *Abstinence* is the first of many steps on the journey of *sobriety*.

It is not uncommon to be dry yet not sober. This so-called "dry drunk" means that, although your loved one is no longer using alcohol, his or her attitudes and actions are basically the same. Beliefs and thinking are still distorted, grandiose, unreasonable, and self-centered. The "dry alcoholic" may also be overly expressive as well as impulsive and volatile. He or she may behave in ways that are inconsistent, unreliable, or disingenuous. To be truly *sober*, alcoholics must change their ways of thinking and behaving.

Listen to this woman:

"Our doctor told my husband Dan that if he didn't quit drinking, he would probably be dead within a year. This must have scared my competent and mild-mannered husband because he stopped drinking. Although Dan was not a happy camper,

I was relieved and jubilant: Now, I thought, we would have a better life together. Well, I was wrong.

"Dan's behavior did not improve with time; in fact, it might have gotten worse. He withdrew into his own world, and didn't listen or share. He got testy and argumentative. He'd pace, be grumpy and touchy, and be just plain miserable. When he was drinking, at least he was usually mellow and passive, and would nod off during the evening. Then he stayed out of my face and wasn't as much of a problem as he is now. I just don't know what to do with him!"

Dan is a classic example of someone who is not drinking but is far from being sober. Remember, alcohol is a *depressant* drug that distorts thinking, influences decision making, anesthetizes feelings, and impairs control. So, when your alcoholic stops drinking, he or she must develop new ways to think and make decisions, as well as to listen to and share, and learn from himself and others. In short, a life without alcohol demands a new way of living.

Fortunately, some alcoholics are willing and able to stop drinking and achieve sobriety. They change their lives—their attitudes, thoughts, emotions, and actions—for the better. They replace "stinkin' thinkin'" with forthright and reasonable thinking, their self-centered feelings with altruistic ones, isolation with sharing, inconsistency and unreliability with dependable responsibility, and spirits with Spirit.

Although they may have had a spiritual life while drinking, recovering alcoholics invariably improve their spiritual lives. Rather than depending on alcohol, they turn to God as the source of their comfort and guidance; consequently, their life becomes more virtuous.

THE "CO-DRINKER" MUST CHANGE, TOO

It's important to remember that the problem drinker is not the only one who needs to change. Becoming healthy yourself is just your first step. From there, you and your loved one are going to have to learn new ways to live and love together.

Initially, more problems may surface in your relationship as numbed and repressed thoughts and feelings begin to emerge and demand from you a new way of dealing with them. How do you respond if your loved one expresses his or her fears, guilt, and shame? How do you act when life is relatively normal? How do you feel when he shares with his sponsor instead of you, or when she no longer needs you? How do you feel and respond when your loved one asks you to trust him or her?

WHEN SOBRIETY IS SABOTAGED

Some people actually have a difficult time accepting and dealing with a loved one's sobriety. They have difficulty accepting and dealing with what they asked for. When issues begin to arise in the relationship, some may even unconsciously try to sabotage the recovering alcoholic.

Such a sad irony—not to be able to live with what they always wanted—is especially likely for people who themselves have not changed. Even though their loved ones become healthy, they themselves persist in their old behavior. They may become envious of the recovering alcoholic's serenity, jealous of his friends, angry at her freedom, resentful of the past. Or, they may simply be scared of the fact that the person they loved is now different.

If you find yourself feeling worse when your loved one is better, you are being challenged to improve yourself. You can honor yourself by seeking help. Remember that your well-being comes primarily from within yourself, not from people and events outside yourself.

As we and our loved ones grow healthy, we will be better able to share our happiness with one another. Being dependent on alcohol or on the alcoholic impedes our building such a divine kingdom. Our challenge is to grow older together in God's kingdom of love.

Chapter Thirty-One

SLIPS AND RELAPSES

"I got scared when Mark started shouting at a party. It was like an old nightmare coming back to haunt me. When drinking, Mark used to show off at social gatherings to the point of embarrassing me and himself. Normally Mark is quiet. But here he was, acting the same stupid way without alcohol. In fact, Mark hasn't drunk for five years, and he's been a different and much better man. What happened?

"When we left the party, I tore into him, demanding to know if he was sneaking drinks, and if not, what the hell was going on. He said that he wasn't drinking, but admitted that he was acting like his old drinking self, but didn't know why. This was not good enough for me, for I drilled him and pressed for more insight. I blamed him for ruining my night, and then shouted a litany of his past drinking faults.

"Looking back, I know that I was just as out of bounds as he was; only my crazy behavior was in private. I, too, reverted back to old controlling behavior; like in the old days, I was placing my peace of mind in my husband's hands.

"The next day I apologized to my husband for blaming him for my faults. I also made amends to myself for selling myself short and for forgetting God. My husband also said he was sorry. With God's help, we talked and listened, and came to realize that we had both slipped back to old behavior. It was a humbling learning experience for us. We shed a few tears, laughed, and we hugged."

EVERYONE CAN "SLIP"

Allison is right on target. Both she and her husband slipped. They reverted back to drinking-centered behavior. Instead of attaching *to* love and detaching with love *from* her husband's behavior, Allison became obsessed with Mark's inappropriate actions. Her having a good time depended on Mark rather than on herself, God, and others. Instead of taking responsibility and looking at herself, she focused on—and blamed—Mark for her miserable time.

The word *slip* usually refers to a temporary regression to previous drinking behavior, on either the part of the drinker or of the co-drinker/enabler. It may or may not involve actual drinking, but the thoughts, feelings, and actions are characteristic of drinking. For instance, you can slip into codependency by needing the alcoholic to change, and thereby try to control the alcoholic, regardless if he or she is drinking.

Such slips for both the drinker and co-drinker are common. In fact, *you* are likely to slip at least as much as your loved one. You might catch yourself trying to "make" your spouse listen to you, respect you, or do what you want. Or you might notice that you are subtly manipulating your loved ones to get them to satisfy your needs.

In the situation described above, both Mark and Allison experienced a slip in sobriety. Something at the party triggered Mark to think or feel something that he associated with drinking, and instead of being aware of and coping with his needs and feelings, he responded as if he were drinking.

Keep in mind that Allison also slipped by regressing into her past dysfunctional behavior. She became preoccupied with her husband's behavior and began to feel anxious and angry. Going home, she aggressively tried to "straighten him out" by provoking guilt and shame. She forgot to detach with love, to let go of manipulation and obsessiveness, and to bond with a Power greater than her inflated ego.

By regressing to past dysfunctional thinking, feeling, and behaving, *both* Mark *and* Allison followed their old programs of drinking and "co-drinking," instead of working their new programs of recovery. They followed *their* will, not a *greater* will. However, give them credit for admitting their alcoholic and co-alcoholic behavior.

When slips occur, they can be opportunities to reaffirm your new and more effective way of behaving. Of course, the sooner you realize you are slipping, the better off you are. A slip is a mistake out of force of habit. Old habits seldom disappear permanently, but they can dissipate when replaced with healthier ones.

RELAPSES

Relapses differ from slips in that relapses last longer and cause more disruption. Relapses are not acute, periodic, or sporadic instances of dysfunctionality, but chronic recurrences, both quantitatively and qualitatively. Whereas a slip may be attributed to a momentary lapse in judgment, a relapse is a more extensive binge that can last for several weeks, months, or years.

The relapse is one of the reasons a problem drinker must always stay on the path of sobriety. Some people relapse after years of being dry and sober. After relapsing, some never return to sobriety; others do.

No one is immune from relapsing. The demons of codependency rarely die and can lure you into their trap. Listen to Martha:

> "It's been twelve years since Matt quit drinking and became the man he could be. More importantly, I learned to be free and serene even when Matt did have an occasional slip. Our marriage and spiritual lives simply blossomed. In a sense, if it weren't for Matt's drinking and my need to fix people, I'm not sure if we would have changed and become happier.
>
> "However, a year ago *I* suffered a serious relapse. Before I knew it, I was my old controlling self. My mother's multiple sclerosis eventually got the best of her, and although I knew there was no cure, I literally went around the country and even Europe seeking cures. Although I had faith, I was actually trying to use God to satisfy my needs rather than to do what I could and accept reality. I was back in my old control mode.

"When my mother was totally bedridden and dependent, I took over. Although a brother and sister offered to help, I did 90 percent of the work. I even refused outside help. My husband tried to help me admit what I was doing, but I would have no part of it. In short, I became exhausted, irritable, and depressed.

"Out of desperation, I joined a support group for MS caretakers, thinking I would find a way to make my mother better. Well, I soon came to realize that I had fallen back into my old patterns of well-intentioned manipulation. Although my thoughts and behavior were not centered on drinking, they were still basically the same as when Matt *was* drinking.

"So, to make the story short, I got down on my knees, and humbly asked God to forgive me for trying to do the impossible. I also made amends to my husband for my 'marital disappearance.' And I forgave myself for beating myself up so much. Although it wasn't easy, I learned to achieve and maintain serenity in spite of and because of my mother's condition.

"I got outside help, let my brother and sister help out with my mother, and took much better care of myself. I also improved my relationship with God, and I have returned to my marriage. In short, I realize that the best gift I can give to my mother is to be a healthy daughter.

"My mother died last month. I have few regrets and no guilt or shame. Even my crazy behavior was done out of love, but I'm glad I got sober; it was better for both of us. My grieving is pure. And I'm glad I'm sad because it means that I loved my mother. Thanks, Mom."

Chapter Thirty-Two

FRUITS OF YOUR LABOR

As we continue to practice principles of sobriety in all our affairs, we will increasingly reap and enjoy the fruits of our labors. In order to do this, we must continue to attach to God and detach with love; stop manipulating and enabling; accept and let go of our illusionary control; improve and nurture ourselves regardless of what anyone does; and freely choose to act in healthy ways.

Perhaps the most reliable, valid, and clearest symptom of healthy behavior is *serenity*. Serenity does not mean that all things and all people are in harmony. Rather, it is a *persistent peace* in the core of our being where God's community of love resides, regardless of what happens around us.

Serenity may be the best way to determine if we are acting appropriately for ourselves and our loved ones. Conversely, when we are persistently upset, conflicted, or disharmonious, we are probably looking too much outside and not enough within ourselves.

To be sure, serenity is not heaven or perpetual perfection. Serenity is a process of building the kingdom within and among us. When experiences challenge our well-being, we can learn to accept, cope with, and grow from them. We come to realize that life's difficult times are absorbed and transformed in the grace of serenity.

It is relatively easy to remain serene while we are living the good life, when everything comes together in harmony. However, while we are on earth, we can anticipate disruption. We can never completely escape unfairness, absurdity, and suffering. And yet, when you have mastered the *art* of being serene, your pain will be less intense and frequent.

Nevertheless, pain is still important, for it demands attention, evokes care, and motivates us to connect with God. Trying

159

times can be signals to strengthen your attachment to God. With God's grace, you *can* learn to accept with serenity what you cannot change, and to discern and choose what you can.

In addition to inner peace, a sense of serenity brings other benefits as well: clarity of vision, relaxed discipline, fluidity of thought, quiet strength, and free behavior. Your thoughts and choices become freer and more efficacious. Furthermore, your attitudes will have a positive impact on others. Your troubled loved ones will no longer be able to manipulate or highly upset you. Instead, your way of being will invite them to call on their source of serenity.

Paradoxically, our dark nights of alcohol can lead to enlightenment and strength. We can come to be virtuous people of God. Through faith, we are able to temper our tendencies to manipulate what is beyond our control. In faith, we surrender to a holy reality that affirms our radical powerlessness and dependency on God.

Listen to this man whose son was an excessive drinker:

> "One of my greatest faults was to lecture my son on the errors of his ways and to make him see the 'right' way—*my* way. I analyzed things to death, and would try to convince him with my infallible intellectualizing. KISS—Keep It Simple, Stupid—was practically impossible for me.
>
> "After much pain for both me and my son, I started to let go of my grandiose control, and to let God be my source of knowledge and direction. An enormous and comforting relief came over me, for no longer did I have to solve the unsolvable. Now I can place my son and me in God's care."

Trust in God engenders hope. As we surrender ourselves into God's hands, recognizing our own powerlessness, we begin to cultivate an enduring vision of infinite possibilities. Even if our loved one continues to drink, we let go of our expectations and continue to hope for a better day, if not sooner than later, then ultimately. Our hope is not wish-fulfillment or magical thinking that everything will be all right. To the contrary, hope helps us to see, think, and decide more realistically, be less frustrated and depressed, and to keep contact with our Source of meaning.

Above all, our well-being originates, is sustained and nourished in, through, and by God. Love for and from God motivates and guides us to strive to love others and ourselves unconditionally. Being within Divine Love enables us to give what we want to receive. Surrendering to the care of God empowers and comforts us so that we no longer need our loved ones to change. No matter what, our love is steadfast.

As we learn to step back and allow God to work in the lives of our problem drinker as well as in ourselves, we will find ourselves growing spiritually and capable of even deeper intimacy. Each time we practice patience, detachment, and humility, we are reminded that sometimes inaction is faster and better than action. With patience and fortitude, we can stand strong in God's love. Accepting our weak and fallen self initiates, maintains, and provokes strength and transcendence.

Recovery for us and our loved ones is not a state or condition but more of a process of imperfectly growing in perfection. As we start to function, feel, and look better, people begin to notice and affirm our renewed being. As this happens, we freely enjoy and suffer what life has to offer.

We come to realize that life is a banquet that will nurture us regardless of what our loved ones do. We come to believe in Divine Providence, that God will provide us with what we need as well as with gifts to enjoy and suffer.

Out of the desert of drinking, we come to the promised land where there is a time for all seasons—a time to control and a time to surrender, a time to talk and a time to listen, a time to suffer and a time to rejoice, a time to act and a time to wait, a time to teach and a time to learn, a time to fast and a time to feast, a time for darkness and a time for light, a time for death and a time for life.

When you love someone who drinks too much, you must keep your eyes on the promised land where you and your loved ones will live forever in love with one another and God. Then, no matter what happens, you live a good, serene, and meaningful life.

BIBLIOGRAPHY

Al-Anon Faces Alcoholism. Second Edition. New York: Al-Anon
  Family Group Headquarters, Inc., 1989.
Alcoholics Anonymous: Big Book. New York: Alcoholics Anonymous
  World Services, Inc., 1976.
Bartimole, Carmella and John. *Teenage Alcoholism and Substance
  Abuse.* Hollywood, FL: Frederick Fell Publishers, 1988.
Beattie, Melody. *Codependent No More.* New York: Harper/
  Hazelden, 1987.
Beattie, Melody. *Beyond Codependency: And Getting Better All the
  Time.* New York: Harper/Hazelden, 1989.
Benton, Sarah Allen. *Understanding the High Functioning Alcoholic.*
  New York: Praeger, 2009.
Berg, Insookim, and Scott D. Miller. *Working with the Problem
  Drinker.* New York: W. W. Norton and Company, 1992.
Co-Dependency: An Emerging Issue. Deerfield Beach, FL: Health
  Communications, Inc., 1984.
Co-Dependents Anonymous. Phoenix, AZ: CoDa Resource
  Publishing, 1999.
Cohen, Peter R. *Helping Your Chemically Dependent Teenager
  Recover: A Guide for Parents and Other Concerned Adults.*
  Center City, MN: Hazelden, 1991.
Collins, Vincent P. *Acceptance.* St. Meinrad, IN: Abbey Press,
  1979.
Courage to Change. New York: Al-Anon Family Group
  Headquarters, Inc., 1992.
Daley, Dennis C., and Judy Miller. *When Your Child Is Chemically
  Dependent.* Minneapolis, MN: Johnson Institute, 1992.
Dorff, Frances. *The Art of Passing Over.* New York/Mahwah, NJ:
  Paulist Press, 1988.

Downey, Michael. *Understanding Christian Spirituality*. New York/ Mahwah, NJ: Paulist Press, 1997.

Fichel, Ruth. *The Journey Within: A Spiritual Path to Recovery*. Deerfield Beach, FL: Health Communications, Inc., 1987.

Hamma, Robert M. *Along Your Desert Journey*. New York/ Mahwah, NJ: Paulist Press, 1996.

Hodgson, Harriet. *Parents Recover Too*. Center City, MN: Hazelden, 1988.

How Al-Anon Works for Families and Friends of Alcoholics. Virginia Beach, VA: Al-Anon Family Group Headquarters, Inc., 1995.

John Paul II. *Crossing the Threshold of Hope*. New York: Alfred A. Knopf, 1994.

Julia H. *Letting Go with Love: Help for Those Who Love an Alcohol/ Addict Whether Practicing or Recovering*. New York: St. Martin's Press, 1987.

Knowlton, Judith, and Rebecca Chaitin. *Detachment*. New Jersey: Perrin & Tragett, 1985.

Kraft, William F. *The Normal Alcoholic*. Staten Island, NY: Alba House, 1999.

Kraft, William F. *The Search for the Holy*. Pittsburgh: Cathedral Press, 1999.

Kraft, William F. *Ways of the Desert: Spiritual Growth through Difficult Times*. New York: Haworth Press, 2000.

Kreeft, Peter. *Making Sense Out of Suffering*. Ann Arbor, MI: Servant Books, 1986.

Kurtz, Ernest. *A.A.: The Story*. San Francisco: Harper and Row, 1988.

Lerner, Harriet Goldhan. *The Dance of Intimacy*. New York: Perennial Library, 1989.

Maloney, George. *God's Community of Love in the Indwelling Trinity*. Hyde Park, NY: New City Press, 1993.

Marlin, Emily. *Hope: New Choices and Recovery Strategies for Adult Children of Alcoholics*. New York: Harper and Row, 1987.

May, Gerald G. *Addiction and Grace*. San Francisco: Harper and Row Publishers, 1988.

Merton, Thomas. *Contemplation in a World of Action*. New York: Doubleday, 1979.

Nakken, Craig. *The Addictive Personality*. Center City, MN: Hazelden, 1988.

Nouwen, Henri J. M. *The Inner Voice of Love: A Journey through Anguish to Freedom*. New York: Doubleday, 1998.

One Day at a Time in Al-Anon. New York: Al-Anon Family Group Headquarters, Inc., 1987.

Paul, Margaret. *Inner Bonding*. San Francisco: Harper and Row, 1990.

Twelve Steps and Twelve Traditions. New York: Harper/Hazelden, 1987.

Twelve Steps of Alcoholics Anonymous. New York: Harper/ Hazelden, 1987.

Twerski, Abraham. *Caution: Kindness Can Be Dangerous to the Alcoholic*. Englewood Cliffs, NJ: Prentice Hall, 1981.

York, David and Phyllis. *Tough Love*. New York: Bantam Books, 1983.

 green
press
INITIATIVE

Paulist Press is committed to preserving ancient forests and natural resources. We elected to print this title on 30% post consumer recycled paper, processed chlorine free. As a result, for this printing, we have saved:

4 Trees (40' tall and 6-8" diameter)
1 Million BTUs of Total Energy
393 Pounds of Greenhouse Gases
1,893 Gallons of Wastewater
115 Pounds of Solid Waste

Paulist Press made this paper choice because our printer, Thomson-Shore, Inc., is a member of Green Press Initiative, a nonprofit program dedicated to supporting authors, publishers, and suppliers in their efforts to reduce their use of fiber obtained from endangered forests.

For more information, visit www.greenpressinitiative.org

Environmental impact estimates were made using the Environmental Defense Paper Calculator. For more information visit: www.papercalculator.org.